SUCCEED IN EXAMS,
TRIUMPH IN TESTS

SUCCEED IN EXAMS, TRIUMPH IN TESTS

Tried and tested methods for guaranteed good results

JEAN ROBB AND HILARY LETTS

Hodder & Stoughton

First published in Great Britain in 1999 by Hodder & Stoughton
A division of Hodder Headline PLC

British Library Cataloguing in Publication Data
A CIP catalogue record for this title is available from the British Library

ISBN 0 340 72811 6

Printed and bound in Great Britain by
Mackays of Chatham PLC, Chatham, Kent

Typeset in Great Britain by
Phoenix Typesetting, Ilkley, West Yorkshire

Hodder & Stoughton
A division of Hodder Headline PLC
338 Euston Road
London NW1 3BH

To Paddy
and both our families. Our thanks to the children, parents,
teachers and friends who are an inspiration to us.

CONTENTS

Succeed in Exams, Triumph in Tests

INTRODUCTION

Who This Book Is For

How This Book Can Help

Questions Parents Ask About Tests and Exams

Who This Book Is For

This book is for parents who want:

- their children to enjoy school
- their children to succeed in exams and triumph in tests
- their children to enjoy childhood

This book is for anyone who wants to help:

- parents help their own children
- children discover the excitement of working at something that takes effort

This book is for children who want to:

- help themselves
- help their parents help them

This book is for:

- parents and children who dread exams and tests

This book will show you how to help your children pass tests, prepare for exams and cope with pressure. It will show you how to encourage your children to develop their potential.

How This Book Can Help

Examination – testing of knowledge or ability (of pupils or candidates) by oral or written questions or exercises.
The Concise Oxford Dictionary.

This book is written to give practical help and comfort to parents and children in these testing times. Children are being tested all the time, even children as young as four. Taking tests and sitting exams can be terrifying. Many parents feel anxious every time their children have a test. When their children are tested, parents can feel as if they are being tested as well. If their children don't do well in the tests, parents can feel that somehow they haven't done well as parents.

Read on

- Adults can create environments that help children succeed.
- As a parent, you can create an environment that will help your children succeed.
- Supportive environments will help your children enjoy their childhood and prepare them for adulthood. This book will help you create supportive environments.
- Safe, supportive environments are ideal springboards for children to explore their potential.
- Sometimes when children explore their potential, there can be conflict. This book will show you how to deal with that conflict.
- Children can refuse to take on any new challenges when they think that what they do is good enough. This book will show you how to create children who are motivated to learn and succeed.

- ◆ When children are at school they need to learn new information. This book will help your children learn the information they need.
- ◆ When children are preparing for exams and tests they need to practise the skills the exams or tests require. This book will show you the basic skills that all exams and tests require and give you ways to practise them.
- ◆ When children are faced with exams and tests they can panic. This book will show you how to deal with that panic.
- ◆ When children are faced with exams and tests they can feel insecure. This book will help you find ways to overcome that insecurity and restore a sense of balance.

When children don't get the results they hope for they can feel dejected. This book will give you ideas on ways to make sure your children know how to pick themselves up, dust themselves down and look for their best option.

This book has been written as the result of our experience. We have worked, and continue to work, with hundreds of children and their parents. We know how anxious children are to please their parents. We know how anxious parents are to help their children. This book is about safe and successful ways you can use to help your children prepare for tests and exams. It will help you give your children the skills to succeed in tests and exams. Our methods are holistic. They are realistic about the demands of family life. Our methods help children to help themselves. Our methods can help you.

Tests and exams are a fact of life for all children. Sometimes they happen at school, sometimes at ballet or judo. Sometimes there is plenty of time to prepare and sometimes tests happen on the spur of the moment. Some tests are optional and some are compulsory. Some are set every week and some happen at the end of a year. Some tests are to check something that has already been taught and other tests are to see if the children are ready for the next step. A weekly test checks teaching. A planned exam checks the children's suitability for the next stage. Entrance exams for schools are planned exams, as are exams with certificates.

Remember

When it comes to exams and tests, keep a sense of balance at all times.

- The results of tests and exams can help people plan positively.
- People who plan positively will be optimistic.
- People who plan with optimism will see possibilities.
- People who can see possibilities expand their chances of success.
- People who can see possibilities in success or failure stay positive.
- People who stay positive will focus their efforts and succeed.
- Success in one test may lead to other tests.
- Failure in one test may lead to other tests.
- Success or failure in a test does not mean success or failure in life.

Many people have been successful even though they have never passed an exam or done well in tests . . . but passing exams increases options in a changing world.

QUESTIONS PARENTS ASK ABOUT TESTS AND EXAMS

Many parents are finding it harder and harder to help their children enjoy school, be happy and be successful in tests. Parents want to make school life enjoyable and successful for their children. Parents today are expected to do schoolwork regularly with their children at home. Children are tested on what they have done at home with their parents in weekly spelling tests, tables tests and reading tests. Sometimes parents are not told how well their children have done in these tests and feel frustrated because they are not sure whether the help they are giving their children is useful. Parents need information and feedback. Parents' Nights are intended as a feedback session but, despite the best intentions of parents and teachers, many parents can leave these feedback sessions feeling unsure and at sea.

This chapter will answer questions parents have about tests. We hope these answers will help you make school life more enjoyable and successful for your children.

1 What are all these tests for and do they matter?

Some tests give information about what children can do. Teachers use these tests to find out what needs to be taught next, so these tests matter to individuals.

Schools use the results of tests to prove that they are providing a good education for children. Parents and education authorities look at these results, so they do matter to the school and the community.

Some tests give information about what school children can go to. Parents decide that they want their children to take this sort of test. They want them to have the chance to go to a particular school.

- Some (but not all) children have to pass a test to get into a nursery school.
- Some (but not all) children have to pass a test to go to primary or junior school.
- Some secondary schools will only take pupils who have passed a test that they have set.
- Some children will have to pass a test in order to stay with their friends of the same age. If they fail the test they may have to have some or all of their lessons away from their friends. They may even have to go to another school.

Tests matter to these parents and their children.
  Don't panic!

- Most children do not have to do entrance tests.
- Most children will go to a nursery school that their parents have chosen.
- Most children will go to their local primary school.
- Most children will be able to stay with their friends.
- Most children will be able to cope with most tests they are given to do.

2 Do all tests test in the same way and test the same sort of things?

Not really; it depends on the sort of questions that are asked.

Test questions can be divided into two sorts. The first simply requires children to be able to learn a string of answers. The second sort of question requires more thought. Children have to show they understand what they have learnt. They must use what they know in different ways. An example of the first sort of question is, 'What is 3 times 4?'. Children only need to have learnt the answer, which is 12. The question, 'There are 3 boxes of cakes and each box holds 4 cakes. How many cakes are there altogether?' is an example of the second sort of question. Children need to know when to use 3 times 4 and that the answer is 12.

3   Are tests harmful?

Tests in themselves are not harmful because they only provide information. The information tests provide should show whether the teaching has worked and whether the children have learnt.

It is important for children to know that a test simply gives information about what they know at a particular time.

Many parents, teachers and children can suffer terrible stress in the run-up to the test, during the test and after the test. They can suffer feelings of panic, inadequacy, confusion, loneliness and fear.

It is the use that is made of the test results that might be harmful to parents, teachers and children.

Everyone – parents, teachers and children – needs to look at the test results and think what to do next.

4   Is failure harmful?

It is important that children learn how to cope with failure. If they don't manage the first time they can try again.

It is important for parents to know what they can do to help their children cope with disappointing results.

Not every parent is confident to help with schoolwork, but all parents can teach their children how to listen, take respon-sibility and improve their work. Children will learn that through their own efforts they can get the results they want. Children will learn that failure can be a springboard to future achievement.

Your children need to know they will feel delighted with the results of some tests but that other tests will leave them feeling devastated. It is important they know that tests are about what they know and not the sort of person they are. It is important they know how to cope whether tests make them feel delighted or devastated.

5 Are tests helpful?

Tests can be helpful. They can help children deal with the ups and downs of life. How you talk to your children about tests is very important. They need to know that:

- there are many opportunities in life. One test doesn't give them all those opportunities or take all those opportunities away
- their education is going to go on for a long time
- everyone learns at different speeds
- everyone has different things they are good at

6 Should I help my children before a test or do the teachers want to know what my children can do without help?

Teachers are very happy for parents to help their children. Any help you can give will be appreciated. When teachers want to know what children can do without help, they will find a way of getting that information.

7 Does it matter if I don't help my children?

Sometimes children don't want any help and sometimes you will be too busy to help. Sometimes help is necessary and sometimes it isn't. It is important that your children know you are interested in their progress and will help if you possibly can.

8 Should my children have a tutor?

Sometimes parents feel worried that they are not doing enough. The school may draw attention to a problem and parents may feel that they want some extra support to deal with the difficulty. You don't always have to have a tutor. A friend or an older brother or sister may be able to help. You will find more information on tutors in Chapter 17.

9 Is it possible to push children too hard?

It is always difficult to know just how far you should go. If your experiences of studying were unpleasant or limited it can make it even harder to know what is reasonable encouragement and help. Some parents are terrified of pushing too hard. Other parents feel it is their responsibility to insist that schoolwork is done to a high standard. Your children's teachers can tell you what standard of work is considered excellent, above average and below average. This will make it easier for you to know what your children should be aiming for.

You can find out from your children's teachers what they consider to be a reasonable amount of work, and what the next reasonable target should be for your children.

10 How can I tell if I am pushing too hard?

You will know you are pushing too hard if you are getting irritated and angry when you are working with your children. You might be angry with yourself, the teacher or your child.

If you feel calm but your children are getting upset, check whether:

- ◆ what you are asking them to do is too hard
- ◆ they need a rest or something to eat
- ◆ your children think if they look upset you will feel sorry for them and let them stop work

Take a break. Do a relaxation exercise (see Chapter 20) and start again.

11 What can I do if I am pushing too hard?

Decide what you can manage without stress. You can take the pressure off. Do a little and notice small improvements. If you do a little often you will find that small improvements add up to big advances. Do the relaxation exercises in Chapter 20.

12 Can I help my children without pushing?

Yes. If you can find something to praise you will be encouraging your children. It doesn't matter how small the achievement is. If your praise is genuine your children will feel encouraged to do more. Avoid:

◆ saying something is good if no effort has been made
◆ losing the balance between schoolwork and the other things your children need to do
◆ only praising your children if they come top

Try:

◆ making time to talk
◆ doing a job together
◆ enjoying a walk

THE BOY WHO FELT PUSHED

Philip was one of the brightest pupils in his class. Even though he was the youngest in the class he seemed very mature at school. In lessons Philip soaked up as much work as he could, eager to take on the challenge of doing more difficult work than the rest of his class.

When Philip's parents talked to teachers they were always told he was happy, hard working and a delight to have in the class. But at home there was a different story. At home Philip was tense, argumentative, nasty to his younger sister and very stressed if he could not do his homework. His parents were perplexed. Family life became unbearable. It was hard for them to understand why Philip was so unhappy. They always praised his good marks and often bought him a reward for coming top. They were worried that if they didn't find some way of helping Philip be more relaxed he would give up. They saw him becoming more and more unhappy.

Philip's parents talked things over with him. They

realised he thought they were only interested in him when he got top marks. Although they hadn't meant to, they had been pushing Philip. Praise for perfection was causing the problem.

Philip thought they would only be happy with him if he got 100%. He hadn't realised they were pleased that he put in effort. He hadn't understood that they didn't expect him to know everything every time, or to always be the best. He hadn't realised they loved him. Because they loved him they wanted him to be happy, not perfect.

13 Can we help when our children are anxious?

Yes, you can. Some children become extremely anxious whenever there is a test. They may develop twitches, become very pale and thin, whinge, look confused or talk in a babyish voice. You don't need to panic if your children are like this. Children can learn how to avoid anxiety. Encourage them to:

◆ eat a balanced diet
◆ do some exercise
◆ have some rest
◆ find activities that are relaxing
◆ leave time to get work done
◆ have some fun
◆ do some revision
◆ be still

14 Are schools always right?

Not always. It is important to use your common sense when you are thinking about your children's education. There are fashions in education just as in everything else. Not too long ago it became fashionable to say that children did not need to know their tables because they could use a calculator. Spelling didn't matter because a spell-checker on the computer could sort out spelling problems. Many parents disagreed with this fashion. They knew from their experience that skills were important. They knew that although modern technology was exciting there are many times in a day when you have be able to work things out in your head. They taught their children their tables and how to spell. They encouraged their children to know there is always something new to learn. They explained to their children that the more they learnt to do for themselves the more confident they would be. They made sure their children used the skills they had learnt. Their children understood the importance of skills. The children wanted to get more skills and they wanted to improve the skills they had.

THE BOY WHOSE MUM DIDN'T FOLLOW FASHION

Ravi's mum was determined that Ravi would get the chance to do well at school. She wanted to encourage Ravi but not to push him. She didn't want to turn him off education but she wanted him to fulfil his potential. She was concerned when he brought work home from school that was full of spelling mistakes and had no punctuation. When she tried to get Ravi to redo the work he thought she was being too particular because the teachers didn't seem worried.

At Parents' Night she tried to let the teachers know that she wanted her son's work to be corrected. She wanted Ravi to understand that it was worth looking a word up in the dictionary so that he would get it right. She wanted Ravi to stop guessing.

The teachers told her not to worry and that Ravi was doing well. Ravi's mother wondered what on earth that meant. She wondered why the teachers weren't supporting her to get Ravi to do his best.

Ravi's mum decided to ignore the schoolwork and leave it to the teachers. Ravi had an uncle in Canada and he enjoyed sending him e-mails. His mum said he would have to have all the words spelt correctly and capital letters and full stops in the right places in any messages he sent to his uncle. Ravi and his mum began to make a list of words that he could use when he wrote to his uncle, to

*make his messages more interesting. Ravi enjoyed the sense
that he was in a family where spelling mattered and words
were exciting.*

15 How can I help my children to learn?

The sequence is:

1 Write down what is known.
2 Look up a little bit more.
3 Write down what is now known, including what you wrote
   down in step one.
4 Look up a little bit more.
5 Keep going until revision is finished.

The secret to learning is to break what has to be learnt into
tiny bits. A good way of doing this is to find one keyword from
the topic that has to be learnt.

Ask your children to tell you what the word means.

Once they have told you what it means you can ask them
some questions. You can ask them why the word is important
and what it is connected with.

If you can help your children understand what the words
mean you will have helped enormously. Don't forget that
dictionaries and encyclopedias are wonderful friends when
you have to understand something.

16 What can I do if my children will only work when I am sitting next to them?

When you are sitting by your children, watching everything
they do, you help them to avoid mistakes. It is likely that, when
you leave them on their own, they will make mistakes. They
need to know that a mistake is an opportunity to learn. If they
have a go you will know what you need to explain. You can give
your children the confidence to attempt something on their
own if you gradually wean them off their need for you to be
there.

When anything new is being tried we are all apprentices and

need an expert. Even adults know what it is like to be able to do something when a trainer is there to give help and keep an eye on what is happening. The person teaching may not know it, but their presence gives the learner confidence. It takes time before an adult learning something new can keep going without support. Children are the same. They can be quite confident while you are there but, the minute you walk away, doubt takes over and they stop. You can help them become independent by getting them to tell you what they are going to do first. That way you will know whether you need to help.

Suggest they bring you their work when they have done a small amount. You can check that they are still on track. If they have made a mistake they won't feel as though they have wasted lots of their time. You will be able to give them an idea of how to correct the mistake quite quickly. When children need you to work closely with them you need to:

1 Break the task down.
2 Ask your children to do just one bit at a time.
3 Check after each bit.
4 Praise them each time they have a go on their own.
5 Check that they know what to do next.
6 Help them to deal with a mistake.

17 *What are the best hobbies for children under 11 that will help them with their schoolwork ?*

It doesn't matter which hobbies your children have as long as the hobby teaches them how to do something independently. They need to learn:

- ◆ how to put in effort without expecting a reward straight away
- ◆ how to do something well for the pleasure it gives
- ◆ how to experiment with different ways of doing something
- ◆ how to have pleasure in other people's knowledge
- ◆ how to learn from other people
- ◆ the pleasure of putting in time and effort themselves, rather than sitting around waiting for someone else to use their time and effort to make something work or entertain them

- how to avoid boredom – the modern child's disease
- how to live life to the full through their own efforts

18 What makes somebody good at exams and tests?

To face an exam or a test people need mental and physical stamina. They need to know how to do their best at a set time, on a set day. They have to be brave enough to have a go. Each time they do an exam they get a little more experience. They learn how to cope with the emotions they feel. They learn how to pace themselves so they answer enough questions. They learn how to sit in a room full of other people who are doing the exam. They know that for the time of the exam they are expected to work on their own.

19 What should I do if exams make my child ill?

Sometimes children are ill before an exam and have to miss it. Some children discover that illness means the unpleasant experience of an exam can be avoided. If children miss one exam they can feel too vulnerable to try the next one. Children who become ill at exam time, in order to avoid exams, need help to develop mental and emotional courage.

THE GIRL WHO AVOIDED EXAMS

Helen always looked pale. Whenever there was a test or an exam she would be ill. If she managed to get into school for the exam she would usually have to leave because of a headache, stomach ache or because she felt dizzy.

Helen was at a school where the end-of-year exams were very important. Children were put into different classes depending on their results. Helen was the exception. Because she always missed exams the teachers had to look at her last year's work and decide which class Helen should be in. Her classwork was satisfactory. Her teachers felt she could cope with the same work as her friends. She was allowed to stay in the same classes as her friends, but she had never had to meet the same challenges as her friends. She had never had to show that she could pass an exam.

Helen's parents were worried. They felt Helen needed help to learn how to cope with exams. They didn't know what to do. They felt powerless in the face of her exam sickness. They were grateful for the help teachers had given but they were still concerned.

They met with teachers to discuss their concerns and worries. They knew that Helen would not be able to get any qualifications if she couldn't sit an exam. She needed help but everyone felt nervous in case they were pushing her into something she really could not manage. Everyone had heard of terrible cases where children had felt under so much stress they had gone off the rails. Helen needed to know how to deal with stress. She needed to know that feeling stressed about exams is normal. She needed to learn that stress is all right. She needed to learn how she could overcome the stress. She needed to know that she could cope with exams in the same way as she coped with other things in her life.

20 Why do children want to avoid exams?

Exams test particular information in a particular way at a particular time. Children who panic about tests don't realise that. They think their intelligence is being tested. They think they have to be perfect. They feel that they could be asked anything and because they don't know everything they will fail or do badly. They are terrified that people will think they are stupid.

If you have children who are frightened by exams you can help them. You need to know what they could be thinking.

They might:

◆ feel exams have taken over their whole world
◆ think that if they don't do well their parents will be upset
◆ think that if they don't do well their friends will sneer

- think that if they don't do well people will think they are stupid
- worry that they won't be able to cope
- worry that nothing they know will be on the exam paper
- worry that they won't be able to remember anything
- worry that they haven't done enough work
- not realise that everyone else taking the exam is feeling nervous, unsure, scared, exhausted and is longing for it to be over, just as they are

Most people don't like the idea of sitting in the exam room, being cut off from their friends. They feel as though they have been put into the lion's den. They feel their chances of survival are slim. A person who wants to avoid exams is fearful of the unusual situation. Even children who can cope with exams can feel fearful. Children who can cope are prepared to be in an unusual situation and try to do their best. They may feel irritated by having to do exams but they will still give them a go.

21 What if my children say they hate exams?

If your children list all the things that are making them irritated about the exams, they can get these irritations out of their system. They might even see the humour of the situation and laugh at themselves. The list might include:

- I can't sit next to my friends
- I hate working in silence
- I need to get up and walk around when I am working
- I could do it all if I had the book
- I think exams are a waste of time
- I think they are unfair
- why don't they just ask me and I could tell them what I know? I don't need to write it down
- I don't see why I should have to do this exam when I am never going to do Science/French/History ever again
- we have had a hopeless teacher so I'm bound to do badly
- I know more than everyone else does but I'm just not good at exams

- I'm always starving half-way through
- I can only concentrate if I'm listening to music

Most of us can remember saying something like this about exams. It is normal to worry and wish exams had never been invented.

22 How can I teach my children to manage their fear?

Whenever anyone feels fear they have two options. One is to give up and the other is to try to manage the fear and keep going.

STEPS TO HELP CHILDREN BECOME BRAVE ABOUT EXAMS

- You can teach them how to be still so they will relax.
- You can let them know that you understand how terrible it feels to be frightened.
- You can teach them how to breathe deeply to reduce the fear. They can learn that physical exercise has lots of benefits. Physical exercise will help them breathe more deeply. If they breathe more deeply they will be able to think more clearly. When they think more clearly they will realise that exams are only a part of their life. They will realise that everyone feels stressed and they will know how they can get through it.
- You can collect some wise or humorous sayings that can be put on the fridge, in the loo, or on a piece of paper in a pencil case or pocket.

It is easier than you think to help children when they are very stressed. If you can stay sensible they will benefit. Don't get caught up in their misery. Think of ways of deflecting their attention so they realise that their life isn't all gloom and doom. Even washing the dishes works wonders when someone is woebegone. Turn to the chapter on relaxation for guidance.

23 *How do I help my children get started on revision?*

A CHOOSE ONE THING

Ask them to tell you one area they have to revise. When you ask them this it reduces the task to one topic. If your child starts to panic the important thing is not to get caught up in the panic. You need to make sure you are relaxed.

B GET FOCUSED

Ask your children to:
1 Open the book.
2 Find the section in the book that is on the topic to be revised.
3 Start at the beginning and write down five words that seem important.
4 Find five words that could be linked to the first five words.
5 Write simple sentences using all the words.
6 Find five new words.
7 Link those new words to the words they had before.
8 Group any of the words together – make links.
9 Make up questions using those words.

C KEEP FOCUSED

Now they:
1 Write down five things they can remember about the topic they are revising.
2 List all the names. Why is each person, place or thing important?
3 Look for any numbers – say why they matter.
4 Write down some questions they think might be in the exam.
5 Answer those questions from memory or from the book.
6 Write down some keywords they can keep for quick revision.

24 What can we do if the notes are nonsense?

Sometimes when you try to help your children with their revision you find that there is not enough information to make sense. *Don't panic.* You can explain to your children that you can't revise something that doesn't make sense. One or both of you will need to find the information that is missing. Once you have found the information, then you can revise.

One of the problems parents and people who work in Homework Clubs can have is that the information that is brought home from school is incomplete. Children are often confused because they don't know what to do. If the children don't know what they are supposed to do there is no way they can be helped to revise that topic. Parents can feel angry with the teachers or angry with the children, depending on who they think is responsible for the confusion.

If your child is given a page of maths to revise you are in with a fair chance of knowing what the questions are likely to be in the test. If your child is given a topic in history to revise and their notes are not very good, you may have no idea what questions are likely to be asked.

Sometimes you might have to write off a test. Discovering bitty notes the night before the test will probably mean you can't do much, but there are things you can do if you have a little more time.

- ◆ A set of children's encyclopedias, even old ones from a second-hand shop, are a good standby. A good dictionary will often help you out of a hole. At least you can help with what the words mean.
- ◆ Check television programmes. You may find that the topic your child is studying is being featured.
- ◆ Ring a friend whose child is in the same class or year to see if your child can borrow their book to copy some notes.
- ◆ Keep older brothers' or sisters' books. They might come in handy.

25 *What do I do if my children say they don't understand?*

When children say they don't understand it can affect you in several ways.

◆ You can feel interested in helping sort out the problem. Children who listen to your explanations or suggestions and then do what they can, make you feel your efforts are worthwhile.

◆ You can feel exhausted at the thought of having to try to help. Children who are not listening to anything you say but just waiting for it all to make sense, without putting in any effort themselves, are exhausting. You are doing all the work. They are giving you no positive feedback. They have no idea that you need encouragement to think of new ways of explaining what they don't understand. They have no idea they should be taking some responsibility. Instead they think their difficulty is your entire problem.

◆ You can feel that you don't want to help. Children can make you feel like giving up. They can seem so hostile towards you and the work that you can't keep going. They can appear totally indifferent to the work. Many children have no idea how their body language affects you. Many children know exactly how their body language is affecting you.

Stay calm. Whenever you feel the tension rise, make a conscious effort to relax. Let your children know how their body language is affecting you. Encourage them to find ways of sitting or looking at you when they find something difficult which will help you keep going. Children need to know that their body language can be as powerful as their spoken language. They need to learn how to use their body language positively so they can get the help they need. You have to make sure that you stay calm so you can be as open-minded as possible.

26 Why do some children always say they don't understand?

♦ Children often say they don't understand as a way of avoiding the responsibility of learning for themselves. What they are saying is, 'It is somebody else's problem.'

♦ They may have missed something that everyone thinks they have been taught or had explained to them.

♦ They don't want to make any effort to work out what they can do.

♦ Sometimes children say they don't understand even when it is quite obvious that they do understand or could understand, if they made some effort. It is a way of getting out of the work.

♦ Sometimes they don't believe they can understand.

27 How can I help my children to understand?

♦ Ask them to tell you one thing they know about the topic.

♦ If they can't do that, look up the topic word together in the dictionary and in the child's exercise book.

♦ Read the definition out loud.

♦ See if the definition reminds your children of something else that they have been taught. At this point they may remember that they have been taught it.

♦ If your children still have no idea you will need to help them learn the topic from scratch.

28 Should I 'hot-house' my child?

Some parents make the decision that they will 'hot-house' their children so the children can excel in some way. Hot-housing is a controversial area. It means that children's lives are focused on one skill or one goal. There is a difference between hot-housing your children and providing opportunities in a sensible way at a sensible time. Every parent needs to think about whether their family life is balanced so their children can thrive. No one can advise you about this. Every family is different. Parents need to weigh up the benefits and the problems that come with focusing on one area.

The danger, if you hot-house your children, is that you

might leave something important out. You might want your children to excel at swimming, school, music, surfing or any of the activities that are available for children these days. Your children might be so involved in competitions or have such an exhausting work schedule that they have little time to develop all the skills people need if they are going to become successful adults. These skills include making friends, setting realistic goals, coping with failure and having fun.

Children who have been hot-housed can be like workaholics. They are always trying to get to some goal. They have no life apart from the goal. They have no conversation apart from the goal and what they are doing to achieve their goal. Some children 'hot-house' themselves. They spend hours on football, horses, computers or their studies. They see anything apart from their goal as irrelevant. They have no balance in their life. Some of these children go on to be successful and some don't.

29 Should teenagers have jobs?

Teenagers have exam commitments but there are benefits to be had from having a job.

Children who have jobs can benefit because they gain independence and maturity. They learn that in the outside world they have a value. They learn that they will only be paid if they are giving value. They learn how to work co-operatively, respond to training and watch other people at work. They learn how to organise their time so they can finish all the things they have to do at work. They may learn the importance of qualifications.

All these things help when they are preparing for exams.

Children who don't work may think that work is easy. They may think that money has no value. They may not realise how important it is to organise their time so that they do the work they are expected to do and get it finished.

Children who do work need to be protected from exploitation and working times that affect their chances to study. They need to recognise that they must balance their future ambitions with their present commitments.

30 Should I limit my children's activities so they can concentrate more on their schoolwork?

Sometimes activities outside school help children do better in school.

THE GIRL WHO MADE THE BEST OF EVERYTHING

Lizzie was eleven. She was always busy planning for some project she had on the go. It might be to do with schoolwork, Guides, making cards to sell for Christmas or the next production she was in at the drama club. Her mind was active but systematic. She used every moment of her time as usefully as she possibly could. She was never bored because at any point she could think about some plan or enjoy going over something that she had already done. She knew how to notice things that were going on around her. She used her eyes and ears all the time and saw and heard things that others missed. She was happy to join in conversations but she always thought before she spoke and everyone welcomed her company in any discussion. She understood that learning was possible in any situation and at any time. Lizzie was always willing to have a go.

Lizzie knew how to see things through. She learnt how to pace herself. She was a naturally enthusiastic and outgoing person who enjoyed variety in her life. Her activities meant she learnt how to organise and prioritise so she would feel a sense of satisfaction in everything she did.

If you have children like Lizzie, who like to have lots of things on the go, you can help them learn how to feel a positive sense of achievement by encouraging them to set realistic targets for each activity. This will help them learn to prioritise and organise.

PART I

MAKING THE MOST OF SCHOOL

1. FOUR-YEAR-OLDS WHO THRIVE

2. HELPING YOUR CHILDREN GET STARTED AT SCHOOL

3. YOUR YOUNG CHILDREN'S MEMORY AND HOW IT CAN WIDEN THEIR WORLD

4. HOMEWORK

5. BEING REALISTIC ABOUT WHAT IS POSSIBLE

6. THE IMPORTANCE OF BEING AS FIT AND HEALTHY AS POSSIBLE

7. THE TRANSITION FROM PRIMARY TO SECONDARY SCHOOL

CHAPTER 1

FOUR-YEAR-OLDS WHO THRIVE

Four and at school

Many children start school when they are four. They might start the day after their fourth birthday or they might start on the day before they are five. There is a world of difference between being just four and nearly five. A nearly five-year-old has lived a whole year more than a child who is just four. And when a child has lived only four years and not five, a year is a long time.

What a four-year-old needs

Four-year-olds need time to grow. Wherever they are, children of four need plenty of time to look and touch and smell and hear and ask questions. They need time when people can point out birds and flowers, dangers and delights. They need time when people can answer questions. They need time to be helped to cope with their different experiences. They need time so that they will feel confident. Four-year-olds love to show others what they know. They need people who are interested and have time to listen. Four-year-olds who are in large classes might miss the sort of help they need to grow into capable, comfortable and confident children.

You can help your children become capable, comfortable and confident with the people and the situations they meet.

Carefully does it – keep the balance

If you only make your children capable they might be able to do everything they are supposed to do but not necessarily in a co-operative way.

If you only make your children comfortable they might be great at chatting to others but not know how to get down to work.

If you only make your children confident that they are wanted wherever they are, they may not have any idea how to become independent.

The lives of four-year-olds

Some four-year-olds will have:

- moved country
- moved house
- had a grandparent who has died
- been adopted
- had a new brother or sister
- had an illness
- had a parent who has left home
- had a difficult birth
- been to nursery school
- had a nanny
- never gone to playschool
- had a parent who has been ill
- had a parent who has died
- got a new stepfather or a stepmother

Most children are trying to cope with something. All children need to feel they can cope. They need to feel capable whether they are at home, at school or playing with friends.

Some four-year-olds will be:

- twins or triplets
- asthmatic
- allergic to certain foods
- disabled themselves or have a brother or sister who is disabled
- cute and adored by everyone
- very tall for their age
- very small for their age
- difficult
- easy

It's good to be capable, confident and comfortable

Most four-year-olds will feel that they are comfortable, capable and confident children. They will feel that they matter, that what they do matters and that other people matter. All four-year-olds have the right to feel this way.

Capable four-year-olds are able to meet new experiences knowing that they will learn from them and will probably enjoy them. Capable four-year-olds are interested in life and open to finding out more. They see adults as people who can tell them the answers to their questions, show them how to do things and give them a chance to explore safely.

Confident children who are four will be able to protect themselves against other children interfering with what they are trying to do.

Comfortable children who are four will be interested in what other children are doing but will not interfere. They can work out whether it is all right for them to join in and are happy to be involved at whatever level other children are prepared to allow. They are good conversationalists because they use their own experience as a way of linking themselves to the discussion.

When four-year-olds were allowed to be four-year-olds they didn't need to be taught how to be confident, capable and comfortable. They could stand and stare, rough and tumble and explore what was around. Now there are different demands on four-year-olds. They are now expected to be like six-year-olds used to be. They have to sit still for long periods, know the alphabet, how to write all the letters and how to spell their name and other simple words. Many four-year-olds now in school spend most of their time doing reading, writing and number work. You can help your four-year-old deal with the challenges that you never knew.

Tips for making your children capable

◆ Teach them to do what is expected of someone of their age. Capable four-year-olds will know how to go to the toilet, wash their hands, behave when out, get dressed, put away toys, play a game, do a jigsaw, use pencils and crayons, play with Plasticine, carry plates from the table, put their clothes away and be safe with a baby.

◆ Capable four-year-olds will still need supervision. Although they are being taught responsible behaviour, four-year-olds need older people to turn to in case they have a problem.

Tips for making your children confident

◆ Have a routine that your children understand. Confident children know that there are some certainties in life.

◆ Confident children know that people have priorities. They know that priorities are important. They expect to be told what the priorities are or be able to pick them up for themselves.

◆ Confident children can cope with change. They know that life has an order. They know that eventually they will work out what is happening. They know they will be able to do what is expected.

◆ Confident children feel that change is interesting, not alarming.

Tips for making your children comfortable – whatever their age

◆ Be interested in what they have to say. You can show children that you are genuinely interested in what they have to say by asking them questions. You need to chat to your children in order for them to chat to you.

◆ Give children words so that they can make it easier for other people to understand what they are saying. Tell them where you are going on holiday. Share with them the detail of family decisions and plans. Give them the chance to tell someone about what is being planned.

There are plenty of decisions and plans that can be shared with children without you feeling as if they might suddenly reveal something you would rather have kept hidden.

◆ Teach your children how to behave. Children who have been taught good manners feel more comfortable than children who are not sure of what they are supposed to do. Your children can send 'thank-you' notes or make a 'thank-you' phone call, when they have been out for tea or have been given a gift. They can send Get Well, Birthday or Congratulations cards. They can send postcards from holidays. They can take their grandpa for a cup of tea. They can select presents to give to people. Good manners and learning how to show people that they are in your thoughts, means that you carve a place out for yourself in their thoughts as well. When children show people that they matter, a trust builds up and the benefits of that trust make your children more comfortable. Children realise that they are not alone trying to sort out every difficulty they meet. They know there are people who will help whether the problem is big or small.

Schools have to prove that the education they offer makes a difference. Many children do a test when they go to school so that any progress at school can be measured. Four-year-olds are being given base-line tests. These tests give teachers information like whether the children can use a pencil, scissors and glue and whether they can concentrate. They may include activities that will tell the teacher whether the children can write or read. They will include the teacher's observations about children's ability to cope with their classmates.

It is important that parents and teachers don't panic about tests. It is important that the education of four-year-olds isn't limited to what can be measured by a test. If you aim to make your four-year-olds capable, comfortable and confident you will have children who are co-operative, can concentrate and can get on. They will be able to do what they are supposed to do, when they are supposed to do it. They will enjoy learning.

CHAPTER 2

HELPING YOUR CHILDREN GET STARTED AT SCHOOL

Starting school

At the moment, most children are in some sort of formal educational environment well before their sixth birthday. Many people feel that children should not have to deal with the demands of school until they are six. They feel the years up to six should be a time of learning through play. The demands of school can be daunting, even for a six-year-old. Starting anything new, at whatever age, is challenging. Parents can share the challenge with their children.

Give your children a good start

When your children start school you prepare them as well as you can. You may feel that you will be able to help because you went to school too. This is true, but don't fall into the trap of thinking that school is the same for everybody. Your memories will help you give your children advice but it is possible that your children are going to have different experiences from you. Be aware. Listen carefully and you will know what they need from you.

When your children start school you might feel over-whelmed. There is so much new information to absorb about the way the school works. There are new people to meet. There are new demands on your time. This is a challenge you can meet.

On your marks . . .

When your children begin school you might feel as if you are losing your children but you are not. Your role is changing and it is still very important. Someone else is taking over some of the responsibilities you had. You will have new responsibilities. You are the parent of children at school. You will have to learn the rules. You will have to compromise.

- ◆ Your children have to learn to listen to someone new.
- ◆ Your children will have to learn the rules.
- ◆ Your children might find it difficult to understand that there are things that you can't change. They will have to compromise.

Get set . . .

Going to school will be demanding even if your children have had many experiences with other adults at playschool, pre-school or clubs for children under five. For the first time what your children do really matters.

Before children start school they can wander to their hearts' content and daydream. They can be excitable and show their own individual personalities at any time. It is expected. Small children will behave individually and people will let them be themselves, as long as they are not distressed or causing distress.

Go!

Once your children start school this changes. Your children are now part of a group. What your children do matters. Daydreaming, excitability and wandering all interfere with the smooth running of the classroom. Your children might feel very confused by this change.

Come on

As the parent of children who are now at school you can help them to understand the demands that school makes. If you spend time reading the next section you will recognise when your children are becoming confused. You will also be able to give helpful tips to your children that will make school life easier for them and for you. Your children will see you as someone who understands how to help them, even when you are not there.

School days – rule days

When children first go to school they will be expected to learn that:

◆ *School is different from home and there are new rules to follow.* Children need to understand that the rules are there to keep everyone safe and happy and able to get on with their work.

◆ *When the teacher is talking to them they need to be listening.* While they are listening they will be learning how to do things so that everyone will be safe, happy and able to get on with their work.

◆ *There will be times when they have to be busy and times when they will need to be still and wait.*

◆ *They have to cope with the school timetable.* They may only be able to go to the toilet at break-time. They may be able to eat at playtime and lunchtime so they won't be hungry. They have to learn to pace themselves and do something quiet if they are tired. They have to make sure they get a drink so they won't be thirsty.

◆ *They have to wait their turn and cope with being ignored or not being chosen.*

◆ *They have to cope with sharing one or two adults with lots of other children.*

- *They have to cope with the noise lots of children make.*
- *They have to cope with the teacher.*
  Suddenly children are in a very dependent position with a stranger, and that stranger has to get to know a lot of children at the same time.
- *They have to cope if they are told off at school.*
  They will learn that that doesn't mean they can't go back to school, it just means what they did is not acceptable at school.
- *Their class belongs to a school.*
  In a school lots of people have to be considered.
- *Playtime has certain rules.*
- *Sensible children take care of their belongings.*
- *They must never borrow anything without asking.*
- *Children learn how to make friends at school.*
- *Things that are negotiable at home are not negotiable at school.*

Can they follow the rules?

Parents worry about what is happening to their children at school. There is so much new information that children can become confused. If you are worried that your children might be confused it is possible to find out from them whether they understand what is going on at school. Children need to understand how schools work and how to be sensitive to what is happening around them. Children who are sensitive to what is going on around them will feel part of what is happening. They will be building up a complete picture of what needs to be done at any time. Parents can help children develop this knowledge. It takes time but it leads to success in exams, tests and life.

Helpful questions to ask

You can find out if your children are confused about school by asking them questions that they can answer. Some questions are better than others.

QUESTIONS TO ASK ABOUT THE RULES

1   When you want to go to the toilet what do you have to do?
2   When the teacher asks a question do you have to put your hand up if you think you know the answer?
3   Is there any time when you have to sit still?

QUESTIONS TO ASK ABOUT LISTENING

1   Has the teacher asked you to take anything to school tomorrow?
2   Did you have a story this afternoon?

QUESTIONS TO ASK ABOUT WAITING

1   When the teacher is busy what do you do?
2   When it is time to go to the hall what do you have to do?

QUESTIONS TO ASK ABOUT LOOKING AFTER THEMSELVES

1   Where do you leave your lunchbox when you get to school?
2   Did you get hot at school today?
3   What did you do when you got hot?
4   Did anything worry you at school today and did you manage to sort it out?

QUESTIONS TO ASK ABOUT THE TEACHER

1   Do you know whether your teacher has any pets?
2   Where does your teacher have lunch?
3   Was your teacher pleased with your class today?
4   Do you think your teacher has a lot of work to do?
5   Did the teacher shout today?

6 Did you have a conversation with your teacher today?

7 What makes your teacher happy at school?

QUESTIONS TO ASK ABOUT THE CLASSROOM

1 Who do you sit next to?

2 Where do you keep the coloured pencils in your class?

3 Who tidies up the toys when you are at school?

4 Where do you sit when you have a story?

5 How many people can paint at the same time?

QUESTIONS TO ASK ABOUT PLAYTIME

1 What do the big children do in the playground at playtime?

2 Can everyone reach the pegs to put their coats on?

3 Is there anyone else who likes to play what you like to play?

QUESTIONS TO ASK ABOUT FRIENDS

1 Who did you play with at playtime?

2 Did you help anyone today and did anyone help you?

3 Did anyone at school or in your class have special news today?

4 Do you have any special news today?

If you ask your children questions like these, they are able to give you an answer even if they are feeling tired. You don't need to ask a lot of questions.

Are you sitting comfortably?

You need to make a time when your children are relaxed enough to answer your questions. You won't get much from children who are watching TV. If you sit down and play with them while they are doing a jigsaw, drawing or building with a construction kit they will probably talk to you about school. You will be giving your children space to tell you about what has happened during the day. It is as much a skill for parents to learn how to ask questions as it is for children to learn how to answer them. School is important to your children and if you keep making an opportunity to have conversations about school, you will keep up-to-date.

Understanding problems

When children have rested they might tell you a lot more. Listen carefully and you will find out a great deal. You might find out:

◆ times when your children have misunderstood some instructions
◆ times in the school day when your children are confused about what they should do and how they should do it
◆ times in the day when your children feel confident
◆ times in the day when your children feel low or tired or unhappy

The benefits of talking

◆ Children who can talk about school will feel that school is part of their life and not something separate and of little consequence.
◆ Children who talk about school realise that there is a lot to learn about how their classroom and their school works. They notice things they need to know.
◆ Children who notice things are less likely to be confused.
◆ Children who are not confused will see how they can help make school better for everyone.
◆ Children who are not confused learn more.
◆ Children who learn more will get more out of school. The more children get out of school the more likely they are to be successful at school and in exams and tests.

Explaining how to focus in a group

There are some things you can do at home to help your children get the most out of school. One of the things you can do is explain how groups work.

Children need to work together at school. They will work in small groups on set tasks. They will be in a large group when they are listening to the teacher. They will be in a small group, maybe as few as two, when they are sitting at a table getting on with their work. They will be part of a much larger group in the playground and in the assembly. They will be expected to move around the school in a group when their class is going from one place to another. When they are in a group they are expected to notice what the group is doing and make sure they are doing it as well.

THE BOY WHO MADE EVERYONE FEEL SPECIAL

Harry was a pleasure to teach and a pleasure to be with when he was in a group. When he was in a group he showed people he was interested in what they had to say. He paid attention when they were speaking and asked questions. He took notice of what they had said. Harry spoke clearly and checked that what he had said was understood. He knew how to behave in a group so everyone could learn from him, each other and the teacher.

THE BOY WHO DESTROYED THE GROUP

Josh didn't listen. He didn't appear to be interested in anything that was going on unless he was directly involved. He was not interested in other people's contributions or particularly bothered about whether they were interested in his. His main interest was trying to get other people to laugh. He would pull faces and make the others giggle when the teacher was talking. He wrecked any group he was in. Josh stole people's chances to learn because he couldn't behave in a group.

Teaching children how to behave in a group

Children need to know

- where to look and how to look
- how to listen and who to listen to
- how and when to move
- when to talk and when to be quiet
- that whatever is happening, they should behave

THE DIFFERENCE BETWEEN HOME AND SCHOOL

In a family it may be easy to give individual attention to your children. Even if it is only for a few minutes while they are getting ready for bed or when they get in from school, you will be able to chat together with your children. You will probably be able to find time to repeat things your children have not heard. You may have time to ask questions to find out more. You will look at your children, reply to every statement they make and generally be available just for them.

In a class your children will not get the same attention as they would at home. In a class most teaching is to a group. Children are expected to listen, remember and then get on with whatever they are supposed to do. There is rarely time for the teacher to speak to each child in the class individually about each thing they have to do. Teachers do not have time to make sure each child has understood what has to be done. They have to give instructions to the whole group.

SHARING THE TEACHER'S TIME

If the teacher is listening to your child read, that means all the other children will be getting on with their work, either in groups or on their own. When the teacher is listening to another child read, your child will be expected to get on with the work as well.

If the class listens to your child tell a piece of news, your child will be expected to listen to what other children have to say when it is their turn.

If the teacher is sorting out a problem for your child, the rest of the class have to wait or get on with some work by themselves. Your child will be expected to be sensible in a group, when the teacher needs to sort out a problem for someone else.

Children need to know that although they are always individuals, sometimes they are individuals within a group. Your children will learn how to be part of a group from you as well as from other people.

A good way to explain how to behave in a group is to compare it to going to the cinema. If you go to the cinema you will be part of a large audience watching the film. You might be part of a group finding a parking space. You will also be part of a small group waiting to buy a ticket. If you talk to your friend quietly while you are in the queue you are unlikely to upset anybody. When you are watching the film you will be watching as an individual. You will have your own responses to what you see. If you talk to your friend during the film you are likely to upset the other people around you. Before the film starts you will not cause a problem if you swap seats or talk. Once the film is showing you will be irritating if you keep bobbing about.

CHILDREN WILL FOLLOW YOUR EXAMPLE

Your children will be learning from you all the time. They will be learning how a group works whenever you are out together and involved in a group.

Mrs Robinson was called in to school. She was told that Jenny, her daughter, never listened in lessons. It seemed Jenny thought the school rules didn't apply to her. Mrs. Robinson was embarrassed when she was told. She left the school not sure what she could do. Next time she parked at the school she went, as usual, into the 'staff only' parking space. As she locked the car it dawned on her why Jenny might be so difficult in school. She realised Jenny probably thought that rules didn't matter. Mrs. Robinson began paying more attention to rules. She stopped using the 'staff only' parking space. She stopped parking on double yellow lines when she thought she could get away with it and stopped thinking of excuses to be served first when she was in the greengrocer's. Jenny got the message. It took a little time for Jenny to unlearn what she had been doing and learn what she should be doing. But it worked in the end.

TEACH YOUR CHILDREN HOW TO OPERATE IN A GROUP AND THEY WILL LEARN TO LIKE LEARNING AT SCHOOL

David wanted people to be interested in what he had to say but spoke in such a tiny voice that people had to work very hard to hear him and know what he had to say. He always looked miserable. He would look down at the floor, look away from anyone who was asking him a question and hunch his shoulders over as if to protect himself. He couldn't understand why people overlooked him in discussions. He stopped wanting to go to school and became withdrawn at home.

David needed to learn that even quiet people can cause a problem in a group. Every person in the group has to try to make the group work. He needed to learn that how he looked at people affected the way people looked at him. If he spoke quietly when he didn't need to, people would give up trying to listen to what he had to say. If he looked miserable when other people were speaking to him they would eventually leave him out.

Everyone has to adjust what they do to fit in with different groups. Learning how to cope in a group at school is an important part of education.

Children who learn how to cope in groups from the beginning will learn more, be a pleasure to teach and build up skills they can use outside school.

Limits help everyone learn

Children who learn that there are limits to the way they can behave are likely to do well in exams and tests. They won't waste their time and energy resisting the work. They know what the limits are and they are prepared to work within them. They are much more likely to get on with learning what they need to know and making sure that in the test they show how good they are. They will know that questions should be answered clearly. They will know that the person marking must understand and be able to read their answers. As your children grow up, what they do in a group can affect what they do in exams.

Children who feel limits are unfair or don't recognise limits at all are unlikely to do as well in exams and tests. When children don't realise that there are limits they are often too egocentric to show their understanding in an exam. They don't answer the parts of the question that don't appeal to them. They often decide which bit of the question is interesting and then write down everything they think the examiner should be interested in. They never understand why their marks are so low, when they feel they know such a lot.

How children learn to like learning at home

One of the things you can teach children is the importance of having a go. Children who learn that having a go and doing their best is an important contribution will feel learning is fun.

Whenever you teach your children anything, never assume that they have understood the significance of what you have said.

Dog hairs in the marmalade

Philip had taught his daughters how to make a sandwich. He hadn't left anything out, or so he thought. He and his wife were delighted when, early one morning, they were told by the children to stay where they were because their breakfast, marmalade sandwiches, was going to be brought to them in bed. The girls were buzzing with excitement. Philip wanted to see the children in action. He crept down to the kitchen. He was taken aback to find that the girls were making the sandwiches on the kitchen floor. He overcame his impulse to rush in and tell them to get the bread off the floor. Instead he tiptoed back to the bedroom to tell his wife that if she found any dog hairs in the marmalade she was to stay calm and see it as part of the learning process. The girls were having a go. They were doing their best. They were being helpful.

Remember that learning is not as simple as it seems

When you stop to think, even simple things are hard to learn. Just to make a sandwich you need to know:

- what a sandwich is
- that you need bread
- that you need a filling
- where the knives are kept
- how to control the amount of filling on the end of your knife
- that you need a flat surface to make a sandwich
- that you need a clean, dry, hygienic surface to make a sandwich!

These are just a few of the things. We are sure you can think of more. Just imagine the skills you need to make a 'BLT'!

How learning at home can pay off

Children love learning at home. They:

- love learning in small steps
- feel successful
- enjoy working hard
- trust learning
- know they can make progress
- love having a go
- keep having a go when you are helping them
- keep trying when they know they don't have to be perfect
- know they will get better

10 tips for teaching children anywhere

1 Break the task into small steps.
2 Let them try the steps.
3 If they get stuck tell them how well they have done so far and remind them of the steps.
4 Learn something step-by-step together.
5 Be supportive if your children make a mistake.
6 Take a deep breath and try to sort any mistake out together.
7 Build their confidence.
8 Give them an example.
9 Teach them how to check what they are doing as they are going along.
10 Show them that you are pleased with what they have done. Put the work on display. Make a certificate. Take a photograph. Let them ring Gran and tell her how well they have done.

Ways to help your children learn something they find difficult

◆ Make your explanations short.
◆ Use words your children understand.
◆ Start by asking your children to do something they can do. It could simply be to open the book. It could be to read out the question. Children need to feel involved with what is about to happen. Children need to feel they can do something already. Children need to feel that they will be able to learn how to do this new thing, and that you will be there to help.

Ways to help your children if they make a mistake

There is a wise saying that every parent and every child should know: 'The person who never made a mistake never made anything.'

OOPS! THE BOY WHO LEARNT FROM HIS MISTAKE

Tim didn't enjoy learning his spellings during the week. The test was always on a Friday. He enjoyed getting good marks, but he did not really relish the work he had to do to get them. One week he insisted he knew he would get good marks. He did not need his mum's help with the practice. Tim's mum was surprised, but agreed because she wanted him to become responsible for his own work. When Tim arrived home on the Friday evening he was devastated. He had only got three of the ten spellings right. He was inconsolable at first but eventually he was able to explain to his mum what had happened. The week before, the teacher had left the words up on the wall while she was testing the children. Tim had thought this meant the spelling list would always be left up when the test was on. He was horrified when, just before the test this week, his teacher took the list of words down. Tim hadn't learnt them because he had planned on copying them from the wall. He wasn't cheating. He just hadn't realised that his teacher had forgotten to take the words down the week before. That was just a one-off. He had learnt a lesson the hard way.

Remember that:

- ◆ mistakes happen
- ◆ we all behave badly sometimes
- ◆ sometimes we can look very foolish
- ◆ that's the way it is. It is not pleasant and we might spend quite a lot of time thinking about how to make sure it doesn't happen again

If children learn to deal with the fact that they are not perfect they are likely to ignore imperfections in others. If they learn that they are not living in a perfect world they won't give up when there is a setback. If they learn that they can make amends for mistakes they won't waste time putting the blame somewhere else. Children who can cope with mistakes are more likely to succeed than children who believe that they should always be good, they should always be right and everything will be sorted out so they get the best.

A MISTAKE IS AN OPPORTUNITY TO LEARN – FOR EVERYONE

If your children make a mistake when they attempt something you have been teaching them, you need to try to work out why the mistake happened.

The sleuth's guide to sorting out mistakes

1 Ask your children what they forgot. Give them time to think and they can often tell you what they forgot to do.
2 See if you can work out which step, in the instructions, you might have left out.

---

3 Get them to tell you the steps they thought they had to make.
4 Give them a chance to do it again.
5 If they still can't do it, check that they are paying attention.
6 Explain what you want them to do and check at the end of each step.
7 Give them a chance to do it again.

Check your children understand when you are teaching

Teaching your children means checking:

◆ whether what you are saying is making any sense to them
◆ whether what they are hearing is what you are meaning to say
◆ whether what you have told them will be enough for them to do what you want, in the way you want it done
◆ why they have slowed down or stopped

Children who know how to get on

Children who can get on:

◆ know how to use the information they already have to work out what to do next. They know how to use the information in a question to work out an answer
◆ can be distracted just like anyone else, but they have learnt ways of quickly blocking out possible interruptions. They are able to keep going because they can keep their goal in sight
◆ can lose their confidence just like anyone else, but they know that if they do something or keep thinking, they might be able to sort the problem out
◆ know that the same piece of information can be used in lots of different answers. They expect to look at a question and find some bit of it that they can answer

- are good at noticing the bits they get right and being pleased about those
- notice the things they get wrong and try to make sure that they learn enough to get it right next time

Keeping up motivation

Children slow down or stop because they:

- don't know what to do next
- can't think of something useful to do next
- have become distracted by something else
- have lost their confidence
- might need a break

5 tips to help children get started again

Whatever the reason for your children stopping, these tips should help get them started again. Have a look through them and see which you think will help. Sometimes only one is needed. Sometimes you need more.

1 If your children are taking hours to read a few pages of a reading book you can speed things up. You read one sentence, they read the next. Keep going like this and the story or the book will be finished much faster and be more interesting for both of you.
2 If your children are going slowly because they hope you will give up, you need to make it quite clear that the work has to be done to a reasonable standard and in a reasonable time. You will need to think about what sanction you will use if they are unco-operative.
3 If your children are stuck on their homework, ask them to tell you what they are going to do first. Then you will

know whether they know how to do what they have been asked to do, or whether you will need to teach them.

4   If your children can't get on with writing a story, ask them to tell you what it is going to be about. Tell them what you think the keywords and the key events are. Then ask them to write down the keywords and key events and see if they are able to get on.

5   If your children are learning spellings, test them first to see how many words they really need to learn. They may feel encouraged when they realise how many they already know.

Your ideas might work as well

Can you remember how you learnt something difficult? Can you remember how you were taught? Do you think it was a good method? Do you now feel confident and relaxed when you remember what you learnt? If you can, it was the way you were taught that makes you feel good about what you learnt. Try using that method when you teach your children. You will be able to offer the same thoughtful and supportive help that you received, no matter what you are teaching.

Rewards

It is important to change the pace when you are working. A change of pace can often feel like a reward. Rewards are pleasant. Adults reward themselves with a special meal after working hard, a cup of coffee after washing the car, a bar of chocolate after paying the bills. Children enjoy rewards as well. Rewards don't have to cost anything. They just have to make people feel special.

There are different times to give a reward to your children. You may wish to give a reward when your children have worked extremely hard. You may wish to let your children know that if the piece of work that is being done reaches a particular standard, you will recognise their achievement with a reward.

It is important to remember that if you are giving a reward you should think about whether your children have done something that deserves it. What makes a reward different from anything else you give your children is that you decide whether what they have done is worthy of some sort of special recognition. A grandmother gave a reward when her granddaughter said all the months of the year. The reward was a trip to the local café for a hot chocolate. An aunt gave a reward when her nephew learnt how to do long division. His reward was a chance to play his favourite game. One mother gave a reward when her son wrote his first thank-you letter without help. In every case, when a reward is given it should be in recognition of a definite step forward. A reward does not have to be expensive, it is just an acknowledgement that an effort has been made. Effort is the basis of success. If children think rewards come with little effort or no effort they will not learn the importance of effort.

Be wary of using food as a reward

Many people believe that children are affected by certain foods. They become argumentative, destructive, silly or sleepy. It can be terribly disappointing for parents to find the children they have just rewarded for something good are now letting everyone down. Children can't help their bad behaviour when they have been affected by what they have eaten. The children who are given a bag of sweets for being good at Grandma's may turn into snarling, fighting, unreasonable tyrants as they eat their way through the bag. Try to find a reward that will make your children feel better, not worse.

YOUR YOUNG CHILDREN'S MEMORY AND HOW IT CAN WIDEN THEIR WORLD

How to help your children make their memory matter

Some children would forget their head if it wasn't screwed on!
Parents and teachers are finding that more and more children
don't use their memory. Some children are almost unaware
that they have a memory. Many children don't know *how* to
use their memory. Most children don't know how valuable
their memory is. It seems children haven't realised that one
day they will have to be responsible for themselves and their
memory will be one of their most important assets.

The memory muscle

You can teach your children how to use their memory. The
more exercise your children give their memory, the stronger
their memory will become. Children should remember things.
They should aim to remember their birthday and their phone
number.

Children who find it difficult to learn something they need
to know have sometimes not realised the power of their
memory. Because they haven't realised that their memory is

powerful, they think that they can't learn and so they don't learn.

Why don't children remember?

There can be many reasons why children haven't realised that they can use their memory when they need to. They may:

- ◆ think they only need to remember things they believe are important
- ◆ be used to having someone else remember things for them
- ◆ think that if they are looking at a page or a picture, they must be doing everything they need to do, to learn; these children haven't realised that looking isn't enough
- ◆ not consciously identify key elements in what they are trying to remember
- ◆ simply not care; they have no idea how much they can learn if they pay attention to what they are doing
- ◆ have no idea how much easier their life will be if they care about the things that should matter to them
- ◆ not realise that when other people know how to do things it is because they have remembered something

Make opportunities to develop your child's memory

1 Every time you ask your children a question, give them the chance to use their memory to give you the answer to the question.
2 If you ask them where their shoes are, expect them to remember where they took them off.
3 If you ask them if they have cleaned their teeth, expect them to recall what they did earlier.
4 If you are reading with them, expect them to remember the word that you have just told them.

Watch out! You can destroy opportunities to develop memory very easily. Don't fall into the trap of telling your children answers. Give them the chance to work them out for themselves. You can give them prompts to help them get the answer, but encourage them to use their own memory, not yours.

Improve memory, improve reading

Some children never bother to remember the names of the characters in the story they are reading. When you are reading together, if you always remind your children what the characters' names are, they will come to rely on you and only read when they have company. They should practise the names before they start to read to you. Insist they use their memory to help them when they need to read the names in the story.

Some children simply don't bother to work out a way of remembering. They either think that they will be told what they need to know or they think they are too stupid to do what everyone else does.

THE BOY WHO COULDN'T BE BOTHERED

Brett thought that doing his reading homework meant sitting at the table with one of his parents. He was quite happy to sit there and didn't mind sitting for a very long time. He would guess at words that he could have worked out or already knew and had no understanding that what he was reading was supposed to make sense. Even if there were only two characters in the story he would get their names wrong. His father would tell him what the name was the first time it appeared in the story. Brett would forget it. He would even forget it from one sentence to the next. His dad eventually got fed up and told Brett to look through the story and find out how many times each name was mentioned. Every time he saw the name he had to write down the page number and the line number so that his dad could check. Brett was reading stories with thirty-two pages so his dad knew this was a task that was reasonable.

The next time Brett read his reading book he knew the names of the characters. He also knew that if he kept faltering over names he had been told, he would have to write out the names and page numbers again. Brett was on his way. He obviously did know how to use his memory, but had got away with someone else always remembering for him.

Some children have not been taught how to use their memory. They have no idea how to use it until they are taught. Other children have been taught how to use their memory but believe that there is always someone else who will remember for them.

Memorising facts that matter

◆ Develop your children's memory by asking them questions when you already know the answer.

◆ Ask them what day it is and once they have told you, ask them what day it was yesterday.

◆ Ask them their home telephone number. You are not asking because you need to know the answer. You are asking in order to encourage them to use their memory.

◆ Questions asked in this way help your children to know that memory is important. There is no debate about the answer. They are just expected to know the fact. They will also learn that there are important pieces of information they need in their memory. They will learn that you think memory is important and that is why you are making sure there is time for them to practise.

Children who expect to use their memory will be confident when they have to memorise facts for exams and tests. Children who are given the opportunity to answer questions when the situation is not stressful will feel comfortable answering exam and test questions.

Family and friends can help your children improve their memory

Children love telling other people about what they have done. Give your children the chance to tell others about their days out. While they are telling the story you can prompt them gently with questions. That will help them to fill in the detail. You can encourage your children to recall who was there, what they saw and what they did next. Each time your children tell someone, it will help them memorise particular events so that they can remember them later. Children who aren't given this opportunity drift. They don't remember anything.

Children who are used to telling a story will know how to write stories that make sense.

ONE BOY AND HIS DOG

Tom was going to get a dog. He knew the type of dog, where it was coming from, where it would sleep and what it was going to be called. He knew much more if people had time to listen. Because Tom knew so much that was interesting about his dog there was scope for others to ask him questions. Each question stimulated his memory further.

Children who have learnt how to tell a story that makes sense find that writing their ideas down comes naturally. They are used to thinking about how something began, how it continued and how it ended. They have an understanding of the beginning, the middle and the end. This is the basis of the logic that they will be able to apply in all the things they learn at school or at home.

Why a good memory matters in school

Parents would be horrified if they knew how much teacher time is spent:

◆ looking for children's belongings
◆ chasing up homework assignments that have been forgotten
◆ following up letters home because children have forgotten the reply slip
◆ reminding children of school rules

Parents would be horrified if they knew how much pupil time is wasted:

◆ looking for someone who has an extra pen because the children have forgotten their own
◆ going around classrooms asking if anyone has found a coat, a bag or a lunchbox
◆ having to see a teacher because of forgotten homework
◆ having to copy up work because the book has been lost

When children can use their memory effectively, to care for their possessions and remember their commitments, they will have more time to learn at school and their teachers will have more time to teach. Their exam and test results will improve. There will be less stress all round.

Use it or lose it

The human brain needs exercise. If the part of the brain that deals with memory is not exercised it won't work when it needs to. There was a fashion in education, for a short time, where children did not need to memorise. Now parents are expected to help children memorise their tables, spellings and facts for exams and tests.

What does short-term memory mean?

Children with a good short-term memory will be able to make use of information they have just been given. If teachers tell you that your children have a poor short-term memory they could mean that your children:

◆ never know where their belongings are
◆ don't get full marks for spelling tests
◆ can't remember their times tables
◆ are always asking what to do next, even when the instruction has only just been given
◆ can't recognise letters or words

What you can do to improve your children's short-term memory

If you want to help your children develop their short-term memory at home you can:

◆ find a poem to learn together
◆ tell your children a message that you want them to tell someone else in the house
◆ ask them to remind you of something you need to buy when you are shopping together
◆ talk to your children about the arrangements for the day and involve them in getting themselves ready
◆ play games, a good way of encouraging children to develop their memory skills. A good game for memory is Kim's Game. To play, take a tray and put several different small objects such as an orange, a tape measure and a pencil on it. Cover the tray with a cloth. Tell the children that you are going to remove the cloth and they have one minute to notice and remember what is on the tray. Take the tray away or cover it up again while the children list or draw what they can remember. You can play this game another way by taking one thing off the tray and see if the children can remember what it was

How Kim's Game can be used to teach spelling

The idea behind Kim's Game can be used if you are teaching your children how to write their names, their address or a spelling list. Start by writing out the whole word. Underneath write the whole word except for one letter. Your children fill in the missing letter.

To start with, you may need to let them see the whole word so they can fill in the missing letter. Select a different letter to be left out each time. Move on to leaving out more than one letter. Keep it fun and keep the speed up and your children will want to keep going until they can do it without looking at the example you gave them. As your children get more confident, they will look at the word less.

It is important not to sabotage your children's confidence by taking away support too early. It is also important not to keep support in so long that your children never learn to be independent.

The support in this game is the whole word. You can be a wonderful support too by cheering when they get it right and play-acting misery or horror when they get it wrong. Make sure it stays fun. Make sure your children know you are impressed each time you see an improvement.

Help your children to learn the things children of their age are expected to know

At some point, probably by the time they leave infant school, your children will be expected to know:

◆ colours
◆ numbers to 100
◆ the alphabet
◆ the days of the week

- the months of the year
- the seasons
- shapes – square, triangle, circle, rectangle
- odd and even numbers
- right and left
- that they have five fingers on each hand

Start early and don't panic if it takes a long time for your children to learn these facts. Just make sure you keep giving your children the chance to be able to use important facts. Each time they practise, they put something new in their memory. They can only use important facts quickly if they are in their memory.

Children in junior school are also expected to learn facts and use their memory. You can help your children to learn and build up their store of knowledge in different ways.

Good memory builds self-esteem

Children will feel confident if things that make them special are in their memory so that they can think about them. Check that children know:

- their dad's name
- their mum's name
- brother's and sister's names and ages
- colour of the family car
- what jobs their parents do
- what hobbies their parents enjoy
- the names of family pets
- the colour of the front door
- where the family went on holiday this year
- where their grandparents live
- where they usually go shopping
- their address
- their phone number
- the name of their school
- the name of their teacher
- their birthday

Your children will feel confident if they understand about time and days, including:

- what day it was yesterday
- what day it will be tomorrow
- what time they go to bed

Your children will feel confident if they understand about the wider world, for example:

- that chips are made from potatoes, fish fingers from fish, bread from flour, butter from milk, etc.
- where food comes from – milk from a cow, eggs from hens, oranges from trees and ham from a pig
- that some places are further away than others
- that all people share the same basic needs
- that not all people meet those needs in the same way

Memory helps children pass exams and tests

Even things you commit to memory when you are very young will still be in use when you are old. There are many ways in which you can help your children improve their memory.

USE RHYMES

Many of us would not know how many days there are in each month without this rhyme to remind us:

> Thirty days has September,
> April, June and November.
> All the rest have thirty-one
> Except for February alone
> Which has twenty-eight days clear
> And twenty-nine in each Leap Year.

Make sure you teach your children this rhyme. They will use it throughout their life.

Use songs

Children have always learnt through rhyme and words set to music. There is the alphabet song, songs for counting and songs for learning vocabulary. 'Heads, Shoulders, Knees and Toes' is a great way to learn vocabulary for the body. Look out for tapes you can play in the car or at home which will give your children the chance to practise and learn. Most of us learnt how to count backwards by singing songs like 'Ten In The Bed' or 'Ten Green Bottles'. You can have fun together and show that learning is fun as well.

Songs with actions and movements teach your children how to remember actions in a sequence. As well as learning how to remember they will learn how to listen, anticipate and keep their place.

Singing games help children to realise the importance of remembering the part they have to sing to keep the game going. Children who are learning through games and music develop a huge store of memories that they can draw on and use as a platform to learn more.

Use mnemonics

A mnemonic is a reminder. Many of us remember the colours of the rainbow by reciting a mnemonic like **R**ichard **O**f **Y**ork **G**rows **B**ananas **I**n **V**enice. The first letter of each word is the first letter of each colour in the rainbow. **R**ed, **O**range, **Y**ellow, **G**reen, **B**lue, **I**ndigo, **V**iolet.

Others learnt about musical notes with **E**very **G**ood **B**oy **D**eserves **F**ruit.

You could have fun collecting mnemonics from teachers, friends and grandparents.

How to learn left from right

Some children are helped to learn left from right when they use their fingers and thumbs. Ask them to hold their thumbs and forefingers out (the forefinger is the one next to the thumb). By pointing straight ahead with the forefingers and sticking their thumbs out at right angles, the **left** hand forms a capital L for Left. That means the other hand must be the right. Other children learn very quickly that the hand they write with is their right hand or, if they are left handed, the hand they *don't* write with is their right.

Count how many

By naming and quantifying, children realise that there are hooks that can be used to improve memory.

Use every opportunity to get your children to count. How many members of the family, how many letters in a word, how many days in the week, how many months in the year, how many letters in the alphabet, how much money in their money box? When you know the number that you are dealing with or aiming for, you know the limits you are dealing with. This is an important aid to memory.

Give it a name

Children need to know words so that they can build on their knowledge. Without words there can't be thought. Without words it is difficult to memorise. Important words are names for things. They are labels.

Use the kitchen as your base and get your children to find ten things in the fridge, ten things in the cutlery drawer, ten things that come in tins, ten things in the cupboard. Can they name each thing? Can they tell you anything about them? Do they know what they are for or when they might be used? It is amazing how many children have travelled the world, know how to use computers and can programme the video, but have difficulty thinking of ten different vegetables!

Learning how to use memory hooks means you are learning some of the study skills to be successful in exams and tests.

Let them join clubs

Activities which help children develop their memory include belonging to Brownies or Guides, Cubs or Scouts, or a similar organisation where memorising songs, mottoes and rules is seen as part of the fun of belonging. Each time they make progress they get a certificate, badge or sash. They may be selected for some special event or special post because people can rely on them. They realise that memorising has advantages.

Teach your children to persist

By doing something over a period of time, children learn how to persist with activities. There may be no set requirement to keep going with the activity, unlike in school. They will learn how to set their own goals and decide on the level of excellence that they are prepared to work for and achieve. They will enjoy using their memory. As they memorise things about the activity they will become more skilled and knowledgeable.

Children learn to persist when they do activities like judo, learning a musical instrument, building a play-house or playing a sport.

Presents to aid memory

Often parents are stuck when relatives or friends ask what their children might like as a present. Here are some ideas for gifts that a child with an active mind will enjoy. They are not expensive but they are fun.

- stop watch
- clipboard
- magnifying glass
- binoculars
- scissors and glue
- diary
- torch

- postcards and stamps
- a collection of things to write with and a collection of things to write on
- subscription to a magazine or comic

- balls of different sizes
- string
- goalpost
- tennis game
- see-through plastic wallets
- goldfish
- wormery
- camera
- tape measure
- compass
- geometry set

Presents to help concentration

Any toys that mean your children have to use their minds are good toys. These toys keep children absorbed and interested in improving their skills. When they use their mind they are using their memory.

- Jenga / Timber
- jigsaws
- Boggle
- K'NEX
- Lego
- Scrabble
- Pictionary

There are many others, and it is worth asking friends what they have found to be successful. Perhaps you could borrow something that is recommended for a couple of nights to see if it appeals to your children. If you lend your children's toy to someone else you will find it immediately becomes more appealing to your own children, even if it hasn't been used for years!

Find what is in your neighbourhood

Children who get to know their neighbourhood will be using their memory. Each time they pass something familiar they will reinforce their memory. Each time they pass something new they will notice a difference in their familiar surroundings.

Children who have been allowed to experience the everyday world in which they live feel more confident when they are asked to do something new. They understand that every activity has its own possibilities and limitations.

Expand the number of ways your children travel. Children who have only been in cars wonder where the seat belts are when they travel in trains. Children who have only been in the family car don't know about timetables. They haven't realised that somebody outside the family decides when the bus, train or tram will leave. Children who are only ever taken to places by car may not learn anything about their own neighbourhood. They won't know which places they can get to in ten minutes and which need a lot longer, if they are going to walk. All children should have the chance to explore. It may be scary for you to give your children the chance to have an adventure in their neighbourhood but try to find some opportunities where your children can have some independence. Going out as a family on a night walk with torches will give you all masses to talk about.

Widening your children's world

By becoming more alert to their own environment and by thinking about the things that they do, children are in a better position to remember what they have been taught. Help your children to realise they are citizens. All children will benefit if they have the chance to think about the world they live in, and the effect they can have on the world around them. They will also be aware that they can be people who can help improve a situation, rather than thinking that nothing they do matters to anyone except themselves.

Children should realise that there is more to life than being top. They will be in a position to achieve excellent exam results because they will realise that there is more to them and more to life than exams.

Activities that will help your children's memory

GO ON A BUS. SUGGEST THE CHILDREN:

- ◆ look for a map in the bus showing the route it takes
- ◆ look for your stop
- ◆ count the number of stops to your stop
- ◆ find out what it says on the bus ticket
- ◆ find out how much the bus ticket cost

GO ON A TRAIN. TRY THESE QUESTIONS:

- ◆ what can you see on the platform?
- ◆ what do you have to be careful of?
- ◆ who checks your ticket?
- ◆ how many carriages are there?
- ◆ how many seats are there in the carriage?
- ◆ what can you see out of the window?

COUNT THE NUMBER OF STEPS BETWEEN LAMPPOSTS.
MATHEMATICS CAN BE TAUGHT IN MANY WAYS

- ◆ if you take smaller steps how many can you fit in between lampposts?
- ◆ what is the smallest number of steps you need to take between the lampposts?

POST A LETTER.

- ◆ use an atlas or a street directory to find out where the letter is going
- ◆ How much does the stamp cost?

TRY OUT SEVERAL ROUTES FROM THE HOUSE TO DIFFERENT PLACES AND SEVERAL ROUTES BACK. CAN THEY TELL YOU:

◆ what they passed on the way
◆ how they are going to remember the different routes
◆ whether they passed any signs showing the names of the streets

DO SOME SHOPPING. CHILDREN CAN LEARN A LOT FROM SHOPPING. THEY CAN:

◆ make a list of the shopping you need to get
◆ decide where to get it from
◆ select the things that are on the list

THEY COULD MAKE A CAKE FOR OTHER MEMBERS IN THE FAMILY. THEY WILL NEED TO:

◆ choose a recipe
◆ check they have all the ingredients they need
◆ sort out the bowls and tins they will use
◆ clear up afterwards

MAKE A PHONE CALL. WHAT A SCARY SKILL THIS IS FOR LOTS OF PEOPLE, BUT EVERYONE NEEDS TO KNOW HOW TO:

◆ look up the number or get someone to write it down
◆ make sure the numbers are dialled in the right order
◆ think what to say to the person who answers

TAKE OUT THE RUBBISH. THIS IS A GOOD JOB BECAUSE CHILDREN CAN SEE THE STEPS EASILY.

◆ do you need to unlock a door?
◆ will you need help to open the bin?

PLANT SOME SEEDS AND WATCH THEM GROW. GROWING SEEDS CAN GROW CONFIDENCE.

◆ are you going to use seeds from a packet or ones you have collected from flowers or fruit?
◆ where do you need to keep the plants?
◆ how often will you have to check the plants?
◆ how will you remember to water the plants?

DUST, POLISH, VACUUM. YOUR CHILDREN NEED TO LEARN HOW TO CLEAN. THEY NEED TO:

◆ decide where they are going to clean and sort out what they need
◆ decide if there is anything that has to be moved before they can start on the job
◆ put away what they have used

PUT AWAY THE WASHING. DECISIONS, DECISIONS, DECISIONS. . .

◆ how many different piles could you put the washing into?
◆ where will you have to put the washing?
◆ does it need folding up?
◆ is there anything that has to be hung up?
◆ will you have to ask where some things go?

GIVE AWAY SOME TOYS. THINK IT THROUGH.

◆ which toys could you spare?
◆ are all the pieces there?
◆ how are you going to pack them up?

Children who have practice at remembering are likely to be children who are successful in life. Children who are successful in life can be successful in exams. If you want your children to be successful in exams and tests you need to make sure they can remember. Teach them to be responsible and thoughtful and they will have a good reason for using their memory. They will:

◆ remember when they are at home and that will make home life fun
◆ remember when they are out and that will keep them safe

- remember how to work
- remember they need to work if they want to do well in exams and tests

Memory links make learning leaps happen

When you remember you have made links. The more links you have made, the more you can remember. The more you remember, the more links you add. The more links children add, the more successful they are in exams and tests.

'Hat' links

1 To spell the word 'hat' you have to know the letters.
2 You have to link the sound of the letters to the name of the letters and the shape of the letters.
3 You have to know about sequences.
4 You have to know that these letters must be linked together in a sequence to make a word.
5 You have to remember the sequence.
6 You have to know about learning.
7 You have to realise that when somebody is teaching you your role is to learn.
8 In order to learn you have to listen and make links.
9 The links you make will come from what you already know and what you are being told.
10 You might need to ask a question before you can make a link.
11 You might have been taught 'cat' and by making links be able to spell 'hat'.

Children who understand all these things will be able to make short cuts in learning new things. Because they will understand the basic principles of spelling, they will realise that if they know how to spell 'hat', it is only a small change to spell 'cat'.

Freedom to learn and learning to be free

Parents who know that childhood is the chance for their children to learn what they will need for life will make sure their children learn to use their memory. Their children will:

- love learning to make links
- love becoming more knowledgeable
- want to find out information for themselves
- want to work out how to link what they have found out to what they already know
- know they can survive
- know they can learn
- know they can think

They will have been given the support they need and the chance to try things out so they can be confident, calm and focused.

CHAPTER 4

HOMEWORK

What is homework?

Homework comes in different forms:

- finishing off work or doing more of the work that was introduced in the lesson
- revision for tests
- assignments set by the teacher
- revision for exams

Homework is work related to school that is not done in class time. Most children will do their homework at home. Some children will do it in after-school clubs. Some children will do it with tutors and some children will get it done in the lunch break at school or even in the lesson before the one when the homework is to be given in.

Enjoying homework

Lots of children love homework. They enjoy the link between home and school. Many parents like homework. They also enjoy the link between home and school. They value the chance to see how their children are coping with the demands of school.

Some teachers enjoy homework. They like to see what children can do when they have time. Homework can bring excitement to a classroom. The contributions from home can be delightfully unexpected and unpredictable. Children get a chance to hear more than the teacher has given. They get a chance to learn from children in the class who are bringing in information that they have found out at home.

The common thread in all homework is the opportunity for children to think individually and creatively about a topic that is being or has been covered at school. Sometimes the homework will have to be written in a book in a particular way, but often there is more flexibility.

Family life and homework

Every family is different and all children are different. What isn't different is that homework has to be done.

Your children might say to you that it is up to them whether they do their homework or not. You need to explain to them that it is your obligation to the school and to them to insist that homework is done. Whether other people in their class do their homework or not is not the issue. The issue is that, in your household, a certain amount of time is devoted to homework.

Once your children can get on with their homework themselves and do it to a high standard, then when they do it is up to them. It is a natural development in becoming responsible for themselves. Your part, as a parent, is to check that the work is done and done to a high standard.

If you don't keep a check on homework you could be taken aback, disappointed or angry when it comes to Parents' Night.

Hints for helping

If your children need help with their homework you need to negotiate a time when you can be available to help. You also need to know what sort of help is needed and whether your children need to go to the library or have special equipment for that particular piece of work. Sometimes children leave it too late to tell you that they need some help. A note to the teacher explaining you will do it together, as soon as you can, will be appreciated. An incident like this is part of the learning process for you and your children.

Building homework into your life

Children enjoy homework when:

◆ they understand what they have to do
◆ they can get the help they need to do it
◆ they have the materials they need
◆ they have the time
◆ they feel as if their homework is part of family life
◆ they know the teacher will be pleased with their efforts

Helping children to enjoy homework

If you show your children you enjoy homework and think it is important your children will:

◆ appreciate the companionship
◆ look forward to showing you how well they can do
◆ be eager to listen when you explain something that they can't do
◆ gain confidence when they can work on their own

If you enjoy it when your children have homework and are interested in what your children have to do, they will be enthusiastic as well.

Beware! If you see homework as an imposition and are resentful, your children may pick up the idea that:

◆ they are a nuisance
◆ they are putting you under too much stress
◆ they shouldn't be asking for help
◆ their teachers are a nuisance
◆ it is just too hard to do

If the homework is too hard to do you have several options, some of which are preferable to others.

1 Ask your children to do what they can on their own and you

put a note in their homework diary. If you do that the teacher will know that your children spent the suggested time on the work and what is being handed in is what they could manage. Many teachers appreciate this sort of information. It may be the first time they have given this homework and they need the feedback.

2 Help your children with the homework and let the school know that it could only be done with help.

3 Teach your children how to do the homework themselves.

4 Do the homework yourself because it is too hard for them. You may feel uncomfortable about this option but you don't want the school to feel your children don't care about their work.

5 Decide that you will get a tutor to support you and your children.

6 Phone friends and ask what they have done.

7 The children copy the work of someone else, with your permission.

The best homework is the homework that can be done by children with a bit of support from parents or older brothers and sisters. But some homework that is set mean the children need a lot of help. This help can't always be given in the time available.

THE GIRL WHO FOUND HOMEWORK TOO TOUGH TO HANDLE

Terri was at a school where they were given history homework each week. The homework was too tough for Terri. To be able to do it she needed to read four pages from the history book. She needed to know how to take notes and to know which bit of the book was linked to the questions. She needed to understand that people from the past were real, but in many ways quite different from people of today. She needed to be able to tell the difference between the past and the present. She needed to know what the words meant. In her history book familiar words were used in a particular way. She needed to know how to read the writer's mind so she could understand how to use the index. She also needed to know how to look things up in the encyclopedia and other textbooks when she couldn't get enough information from her own textbook. Finally Terri needed to know how to construct an essay to include the information that was necessary and put it in an order that could be understood. Terri was nine and her mum only had one night when she could help her with this homework.

Courage in adversity

If you have children who are set homework that is way beyond their capabilities, try to find *something* they can do in the homework. Children who feel they can find something they can manage in their homework will look for something they can manage in a test or an exam. Children who learn to think about what they can do are children who will build towards success in exams and tests. They are building their courage as well as their knowledge. Children who feel that hard work is beyond them won't try when they see something that looks like it is too hard for them.

Finding something for Terri to do

Terri's parents would need to decide what they felt was appropriate so that Terri could consolidate skills she already knew and learn something new.

- ◆ They could read the pages to her or with her.
- ◆ They could ask her what different words meant.
- ◆ Terri could list dates and write what happened on those dates.
- ◆ She could name the key people and list the key events and why they mattered.

- ◆ Terri could try to write the essay herself with her parents giving her guidance if she was stuck.
- ◆ Terri's parents could write the essay with her and make it a joint effort.

No need to nag

Arguments can start when there is stress. Most parents hate to hear themselves or their partner nagging at their children to get on with the homework. You start to nag when you forget you are a person and think you are only a parent. You start to nag when you forget your children are people and think the only thing they need do is get on with their homework. Parents and children love to feel that home is a place of peace and not a war zone.

Stress can be left at the front door if everyone in the household is respected and allowed to be a person first and a parent or a child second. When individual members of the family feel they are people first, rather than doers of homework, breadwinners, makers of dinner, washer-uppers or helpers with homework, they are able to respond to each other without irritation.

Being in a fit state to do homework

Children who are in a fit state to do homework feel physically comfortable, emotionally secure and that they know enough to tackle the work and recognise that the work needs to be done. Children who are in a fit state will enjoy homework and take responsibility for getting it done.

CHAPTER 5

BEING REALISTIC ABOUT WHAT IS POSSIBLE

Be realistic about your own limitations

Modern life is frantic. You rush to work, wait in queues that are longer than you expected, try to get to the school concert, remember to let your own parents know you care about them, check the fax machine, listen to the messages on the answerphone and pay the bills. On top of that you have to get the kids to ballet lessons, swimming lessons, do their homework, and occasionally they smile in your direction so you know it is all worthwhile. Oh yes, and then there's tea! With all the pulls on your time and with all the goodwill in the world, time to help your children is limited. You know you could be very successful, and they would benefit from your help, if only they could be ready to work when you are.

Life isn't perfect

Full of good intentions, you let your children know that you will be able to help them with their revision after tea. The dishes are cleared away, the table is tidied, and you sit down ready to do your very best to help. Then it starts . . .

◆ the maths book has been left at school so maths can't be done
◆ you didn't do Spanish when you were at school so you can't help with that
◆ the history revision can't be done from the notes in the exercise book

What had started as a pleasant and productive time in your mind has turned into a 'no-win' situation. *Beware*. Don't make it worse. Try to avoid an argument. A slanging match will just make everybody even more stressed. Take yourself away from the situation for a few minutes, calm yourself and give yourself space to think.

See problems from your children's point of view

There are several reasons why children make sure they can't do homework. They:

- don't see it as important
- think they can't do it
- can't cope with feeling stupid
- can't cope with the enormity of it all
- can't see anything positive about what they have to do
- feel it is pointless
- have tried it lots of times and can't seem to learn how to do it
- feel that no matter how hard they try they won't do it well
- would rather be doing something else
- feel they can get away with it if they don't do it
- don't realise that it matters
- think that if something is hard it should be avoided
- don't realise that quite a few other people will be finding it hard
- only want to do things that are easy
- don't know how to plan their time
- see the task as endless and impossible

This is normal. Even adults can find many reasons for not wanting to get on and do what has to be done. Adults also have ways of getting started. Part of growing up is learning how to get yourself started on something you don't want to do.

How to get started, gradually

You may be someone who knows that if you:

- make a cup of coffee

- sit in a particular place
- have a bath
- tidy your desk
- or go for a jog

you will get started. You will have cleared a space in your head to get yourself ready for the work you have to do. Unlike children, you also know from experience that if you get started you will probably do the work well and you can stop worrying about getting the work done.

Children have to learn what we have learnt from experience. They have to learn for themselves that life is easier if you get started on what you have to do, and get it done. Children haven't developed rituals that will get them going. What they have often done is develop rituals that avoid getting started at all. For instance, adults might watch television for a few minutes before they start work but children can lose themselves in what they are watching and forget everything else.

Techniques for getting children going when they would much rather do something else

1 If your children won't sit down when you ask them to, but keep playing their game or wander around aimlessly saying they are getting ready, you can help them to change direction.

✔ Ask them to come and sit down. If they don't come when you ask, go to them, make eye contact with them and insist that they come with you to the table.

✔ Put the timer on and let them know that when it goes off they must be ready to sit down and start work. Let them know how long they have.

✔ Encourage your children to take their homework out of

their bags when they get home from school and put it on the table where they are going to work. You will have reminded them that, at some point, time must be found to do the work.

2 Clear the table and clear your mind. These exercises, which you can do with your children, will mean you can all start work with a clear mind.

✔ This exercise refreshes the eyes as well as clearing the mind. Put your elbows on the table and cover your eyes with your hands. Have the tips of your fingers on your forehead, your thumbs on the edge of your eyebrows and the heel of your hand resting on your cheekbones. The aim is to block out the light without touching your eyes. Resting in that position, with your eyes closed, imagine you are seeing dark. Notice your breathing and try to make it deeper. Stay in that position for a few moments until you feel yourself becoming calm. Open your eyes and you will notice that the world seems brighter and you are ready to get on.

✔ Put on a relaxation tape or some calming music and lie alongside your children on the floor without touching. Feel the weight of your body pressing down on the floor, the touch of your clothes on your skin. Notice your breathing and let it deepen. Go still. When you feel you are calm and your children are calm you will all be ready to begin the work. If you feel it is helpful you can leave the music on. This exercise can also be done sitting on a chair. Make sure your feet are flat on the floor and your back is straight.

3 If you have children who squirm or slouch or look everywhere except at their work, these exercises and suggestions will help them control their body. When you can control your body you can control your mind. When your body is out of control you are unlikely to

be able to focus on the work you need to do.

✔ Stand facing your child and both of you stand with your feet slightly apart so that your weight is distributed evenly on both feet. Breathe deeply. Roll your shoulders back five times. Then roll your shoulders forward five times. When you have done that shake your arms. Sit down to begin work and see if your child can now focus.

✔ Stand together with both feet on the floor slightly apart. When you are both still each of you bend your leg to lift your foot off the floor. Try to stand on one foot for as long as you can. Then try to stand on the other foot as long as you can. Your child will learn physical balance. Sometimes it helps if you hold your arms out to the side. Shake each leg before you sit down to work.

✔ Children who find it difficult to keep still enjoy this game. They lie on the floor and you start to count to ten. As soon as they move you begin again. When you get to ten tell them how clever they have been and ask them to come quietly to the table and start their work.

✔ Children need to have their feet flat on the floor or on a box when they are working at a table.

✔ Children need to have one hand holding the paper when they are writing.

✔ Children need to have fresh air in the room when they are concentrating.

Take a break

Parents and children agree that breaks are important when they are working. They help everyone. What parents and children sometimes don't agree about is what can be done in the break. If you have a list of agreed activities you won't turn the break into a stressful situation. If you have an agreed time for the break you will avoid frustration.

30 breaks for all occasions

As a break you could:

1 Have a drink of water.
2 Open the window and take some deep breaths.
3 Have a stretch.
4 Lie down and listen to some music.
5 Go out and have a short play.
6 Make a phone call.
7 Read a book.
8 Watch a bit of a videoed programme.
9 Have a chat to another family member.
10 Have a short sleep.
11 Draw a picture.
12 Do a jigsaw.
13 Do some colouring in.
14 Do some eye exercises.
15 Do some relaxation.
16 Go for a walk.
17 Have a foot massage.
18 Do some skipping with or without a rope.
19 Throw a ball against a wall.
20 Practise shooting at a basketball net or goal posts.
21 Hit a tennis ball on a string.
22 Do some cutting and pasting.
23 Write a letter.
24 Feed a pet.
25 Tidy your workspace ready to start afresh.
26 Play with a favourite toy or game for five minutes.
27 Have a bite to eat.
28 Go for a swim.
29 Kick a football.
30 Write a postcard.

CHAPTER 6

THE IMPORTANCE OF BEING AS FIT AND HEALTHY AS POSSIBLE

Comfort zones

The comfort of children at school can affect their physical comfort at home. Everyone needs time to:

- GO TO THE TOILET

  Some of us went to schools that had terrible toilets and we can understand why children might wait until they get home. You might want to give your children some advice about the importance of going to the toilet during school time. You might be able to suggest ways they can avoid any embarrassment when they need to go. Some children carry toilet paper, which gives them extra confidence that they are properly prepared.

  Children who are desperate to go to the toilet may well be irritable when you collect them from school. Older children will burst through the front door, charge to the toilet and only when they emerge be able to have a sensible conversation. Bear this in mind. Don't feel hurt and don't suggest they start their homework until they have found relief.

- Eat

In many schools little learning happens because the pupils are hungry. It's hard to believe that children who eat a lot could actually be hungry. Not all parents and teachers realise children who whinge are probably hungry. Learning makes you hungry and some children are hungry all of the time.

Children growing up and adults who are going to use a lot of energy need a balanced and wholesome diet to keep going. Some foods can keep us going for a long time. Other foods are nice to eat but have little in them to keep energy levels high. Experts know that to get the best performance from the human body and brain, a balanced diet must be eaten. For some families a balanced diet is a rarity, or even unknown, and children eat snack foods all day long. They never have the satisfaction that comes from eating a well-balanced meal. They might have a biscuit, a fruit yogurt or a piece of fruit but still be hungry because the hunger they have is for something filling.

For some children, what should just be seen as party or picnic food is actually their main diet; their main diet is snack food. A snack is something you have between meals or because of some special event. When fast foods were introduced people welcomed the freedom that these foods allowed. At first most families still had regular meals which were well balanced and fast foods were a treat. Now fast foods are eaten more often because of the pressure of time.

If you are using fast foods a lot, keep an eye on the ingredients. Some people can be badly affected by even the tiniest amount of additives. Many fast foods contain much more sugar than you would find in a recipe if you were making the same food yourself at home. Sugar is seductive and children will be drawn to foods like sweets that have made them feel good, even if they are not doing them any good at all.

- Rest

  Some people like to rest by 'vegging out' in front of the television and others rest by doing something quiet on their own, like reading or drawing. Some like to rest by having a chat and others like to do something physical like digging in the garden, riding a bike, kicking a football or working out on an exercise machine. Your children will appreciate being able to have time to unwind in their own particular way.

  After your children have unwound and before they start homework, they should get back into balance. If their rest has been inactive they should do something energetic. A quick walk would do or a few stretches in the fresh air. If their rest has been energetic they need to do something quiet and peaceful before starting on their work.

- Exercise

  Healthy people need to be able to run, jump, stretch and compete against somebody else or themselves to improve their body strength or fitness. For many children schools are becoming more and more physically restrictive. Classes are bigger, children are bigger (just look at the number of children who are as tall or taller than their parents) and playtimes are shorter. Children need to play. Children need to shout. They need to be able to run wildly but safely without driving other people mad. They need to be able to climb and rough and tumble. Some children get this chance in their families but increasingly many children don't.

  Many schools are limiting the range of activities offered to pupils because they don't want to run the risk of accidents or parental complaint. Most children need planned exercise, even if they are very energetic, whenever they get the chance. It is natural for people who are healthy to use their bodies in many different ways. Give your children the chance to let off steam and use up their energy. This will help them get ready to focus on their homework.

Emotional needs of children at school

Many things can upset children emotionally. Something can go wrong at school. They may have problems with friends at home or they might have a brother or sister who makes them feel stupid.

WHAT A SHAME IF YOU ONLY BLAME

Whenever your children have an emotional problem they need to feel supported. The best support is advice on how to sort the problem out. Blaming other people for their distress will not help your children. Neither will giving them a treat to compensate.

CARING BY SHARING

Your children need to know that you won't have all the answers. Sharing your thoughts about their problems with them can help them understand this. Sometimes you won't have a clue what to do, but a hug and a chat and a break before getting on with homework is sensible. You will build up problems for later if you try to make things better by deciding that the homework doesn't need to be done.

EVERYTHING PASSES

Children need support to get their homework done, even when they feel miserable. Misery is usually temporary. If they haven't done their homework because they felt miserable, they might fall behind, get a detention or feel embarrassed.

SAFETY NET

There will be times when your children can't do their homework because of an emotional reason. If you encourage them to keep going when they can, you will be encouraging a sensible approach to work that has to be done, without turning your children into unfeeling automata.

Children are social animals. Social animals have to work out how they can organise themselves. They need to think about protection, planning and public relations.

Schools are social places.

Friendship at school

Most children like to feel they have friends. Some children need approval from their friends. Their friends can have a lot of influence over them. Many children only feel comfortable at school if they have one or two close friends. Some children, who need their friends, would rather be silly in a class and get into trouble with their teacher and parents than risk losing their friends. They feel their friends are the only anchor they have to protect them. Teach your children that the teacher can be an important anchor too.

Problems happen

School is a place that feels full of problems to many children. Children who are quite able to cope in lots of other situations can come unstuck at school. Don't panic. Many children will have a bad year in the course of their school-life when they may be ill, in trouble a lot, not pay attention, not like the teacher or find the work too hard. Don't feel as if their whole school life is in jeopardy.

Understanding the point of school

Schools are communities. They are communities of learning. Children who are fulfilling their potential understand why schools are there and why they are in school. They understand the need to have rules to protect their opportunities to learn.

Children who are failing to fulfil their potential may feel the rules are not protecting their opportunities to learn. They may be in a class with children who have misunderstood the purpose of school and are therefore likely to disturb the learning environment. Some children who disturb the learning environment think they are in school because school is a social place. They think school has been provided as a place for them to meet their friends. These children have misunderstood the purpose of school. They have forgotten, or never realised, that what they do has an effect on other people. If they are talking or being silly in class they think their behaviour is irrelevant. If they get into trouble they feel aggrieved. When the teacher is trying to re-establish the learning environment the pupils feel that the teacher is interfering or being unfair.

Organisations have to be arranged so they are fair to all the individuals in them. Schools are organisations. All children need to know how to help the school be fair to everyone. Schools must be a place where people can learn and teach. That learning environment has to be protected for everyone. If children are disruptive, they weaken or wreck the learning environment and that isn't fair. If children are co-operative they support and strengthen the learning environment and that is fair.

How to help your child fit in at school

Schools are set up to help all the children who attend them. Although your children are your priority they must fit into the school's priorities. Schools will help children who are struggling in any area of school life. Children who try to help themselves will be helping teachers to help them. Everyone needs to see that they are a part of a community working together to help learning for all.

One way you can help your children get the best out of school is to help them understand how they fit in to their family, their school and any clubs they belong to. Everyone has a picture in their mind of who they are. To begin with, it is a picture in outline only. There is no colour. It can be coloured in. Some children can use many colours for their picture. Other children don't know they have a picture. Yet other children know they have a picture but don't realise they can add the colour. If you want your children to see their lives as rich and varied in colour, let them know they are:

◆ loved
◆ part of a family
◆ part of a team
◆ part of arrangements

Then, when they go into a new situation, they will feel that they can cope.

By making sure that you are paying attention to the fundamentals your children need for every situation, you will be giving them support for the particular situation of homework. Your children will feel happier and will be able to do their homework without fuss and without you needing to nag.

CHAPTER 7

THE TRANSITION FROM PRIMARY TO SECONDARY SCHOOL

From the top to the bottom – all you need to know to soften your child's landing at secondary school

It can be shattering for some children to go from the top of junior school to the bottom of secondary school. Parents hope that their children's time at secondary school will be positive in every way. They know there could be a few hiccups but they hope they will be small ones. If your children can transfer to secondary school smoothly, that is a bonus. The transfer can be straightforward and sometimes spectacular. Occasionally the transfer can be tricky. If it gets tricky don't despair. Every problem can be solved once your children know what to do.

Helping children succeed in secondary school

Secondary school is the place where children grow from childhood to adulthood. When they go in at Year 7 they can feel very young and uncertain. The friendships they make and the adults they meet will have a big influence on them for many years after they leave school. When they leave at sixteen plus they should be ready to cope with life to come.

Choosing a school

- Each school has its champions who can quote many reasons why parents should be happy to send their children to that particular school.
- Each school has its detractors who can tell stories of children who were not understood by the school and who didn't do as well as they should have at that school.
- Most schools will benefit children.
- Be realistic. It is unlikely that every school can overcome the problems of any child who comes through its doors.
- There will be strengths and weaknesses in all schools.
- Listen to what others tell you, but then go and look for yourself.
- Choosing a secondary school can be an anxious time for parents. Children need to be consulted. Listen carefully. They may be less experienced than you, but you will be surprised by what they understand. Leave time for discussion and take time to make the choice. The school you choose together is going to be their workplace for the next five years and possibly longer.

LOOKING ROUND A SCHOOL: REMEMBER TO ASK QUESTIONS

Most secondary schools have an open evening when prospective pupils and their parents have an opportunity to look around the school, see examples of work and talk to teachers and pupils. Most schools will allow parents to make appointments to visit at other times, if they are unable to attend the open evening. Never be afraid to ask. It is better if you take an active interest when you are touring the school. You will find that you pay attention to detail. You will become aware of the little things that tell you about the philosophy and the ethos of the school. Some schools have a very high profile in the community and are popular with many parents. You may feel that other schools are second rate in comparison. *Beware*. Schools change, teachers come and go, and your children might thrive in a different environment to the one offered by the school everyone thinks is the best. A checklist will help you make an informed judgement about different schools.

It is a good idea to write down what your children think they want from their secondary school. You can add in what you think is important. Discuss the list with them. Make sure that along with all the other things you are checking, you look out for what your children want. Many parents and children have been surprised by their visits to different schools. They have chosen a totally different school at the end of their visits to the one they thought they would choose at the beginning.

Checklist for the visit

Bear in mind questions such as:

◆ Are the teachers friendly?
◆ Are the children polite?
◆ Are the pupils and teachers enthusiastic?
◆ Are the school clubs available for every age group?
◆ Are the playground facilities good?
◆ Are the toilets clean and fresh?
◆ Are the eating facilities comfortable?
◆ Does the school have a well-stocked library?
◆ Does the work on the walls look as though pupils have done it? Is it to a high standard? Does it look like every child gets a chance to have some work on the walls?
◆ Does the school's discipline policy seem clear and fair?
◆ Does the school have a good exam record, particularly in the subject areas your children enjoy?
◆ Does the school take pride in itself?
◆ Is there evidence that the school is involved in the local community?

- Is there information on how children who are ill, bereaved or under stress will be supported and enabled to continue their studies?
- What achievements has the school had in the last three years – sport, debating, art, science, environmental projects?
- What are the school's priorities and aims for the future?
- How can parents become involved in the life of the school?

Preparing for secondary school

The practical preparations are the easiest ones to sort out: where the bus goes from, buying the uniform, sorting out equipment and getting a haircut. The 'Now you are on your own . . .' preparations are a little more difficult: making new friends, steering clear of bad influences, making a good impression, working out how to join clubs and teams, keeping safe, not being vulnerable with other people.

It is a good idea to prepare your children for the transition from primary to secondary school, but you won't know how well the transition is going for a couple of weeks. In those first few weeks there are so many things that can go right and children are protected from many of the difficulties. New subjects can excite them. Most children will be thrilled by the new freedoms they are given and delighted with their new friendships.

Starting at secondary school

Most children will have gone to a small primary school where they knew all the children and all the teachers. In secondary school, children will find there are few familiar faces. For some children this can be exciting but for others it is terrifying.

James had loved being a big fish in a small pool. He had always been quick at primary school. He was a whiz at maths because he knew his times tables and when to use them. He had a great imagination and his stories were often read out to the rest of the class. He watched lots of factual programmes and often had the answer to a question or could provide extra information whenever the teacher mentioned a new topic. He was one of the best readers in the class and he was quite good at sport.

In secondary school things were different. James felt he had lost the special position he had always had at primary school. Teachers had lots of new children to get to know. The teachers at secondary school didn't know how good he was. He was used to people knowing he was one of the best. He wasn't a show-off. It was just that the teachers at primary school always knew they could rely on him to do things for them, whether it was entering a competition or reading out loud in assembly. He was totally unprepared for the change. He wasn't flexible enough to cope with the new system and he began to give up. He felt at sea. His behaviour changed. He became surly and argumentative at home and even began to get detentions at school.

The tables turn

Some children who are bright and get on well in primary school find the change to secondary school very difficult to handle. While they were in primary school their good ideas and their quick understanding of new information meant that they were always seen as one of the cleverest in the class. They never found anything difficult so they missed the chance of learning how to learn. They thought clever people could do things quickly and because they could do things quickly, they knew they must be clever.

At secondary school most children, no matter how clever they are, have to work if they want to understand all the subjects they are expected to do. The children who have done well in primary school, without difficulty, have a certain natural ability. In secondary school natural ability is not enough. Pupils have to be able to apply themselves to their schoolwork if they want to do very well.

If your children are struggling, like James, to adjust to being little fish in a big pool you can help.

---

4 tips to help children who like to do well

Try to put everything in the form of a question so that your children are working out what they need to be noticing and doing, in order to make the best of secondary school. You can't do it for them and it is unfair to create the illusion that you can.

1 YOUR CHILDREN NEED TO KNOW THAT SECONDARY SCHOOL IS A FRESH START

Why? If your children have always been the best, they may think that they can be the best in secondary school by just doing the same things they did before. They need to know that they must be alert to what it is that will make them successful at secondary school. They need to find out what they can't do and learn how to do it. It might be listening carefully, following instructions, getting on with work quickly or not racing ahead when they only have half the information.

Try asking them if they have noticed anything different from what they had expected. What are the things that have surprised them? Have they noticed something that someone else has or does that they think might make their life easier?

---

2 MAKE SURE, WHEN YOU PRAISE YOUR CHILDREN, YOU
ARE PRAISING THEM FOR GENUINE EFFORT

Why? Children who have been top have often been praised
for almost anything they do, whether it has taken effort or
not. They can feel deflated in secondary school if this
praise doesn't keep happening. If you praise them for
genuine effort rather than for things being right, you
encourage them to understand that learning takes time
and effort.

*Try listing with your children the sort of things teachers in
secondary school may be looking for in an outstanding piece of
work. Your children will then know what to check in their own
work. They will have a better understanding of how teachers award
marks.*

3 YOUR CHILDREN NEED TO COPE WHEN THEY DON'T
KNOW EVERYONE AND EVERYONE DOESN'T KNOW
THEM

Why? In the smaller situation of a primary school some
children have enormous confidence and are very successful
in their work because of this. When they get to secondary
school they are unprepared for the feeling of anonymity
they experience. They can't bear changing lessons all the
time and having to deal with the different demands that
each subject and each teacher makes.

*Try letting your children do the supermarket shopping for you. They
can have the list and the money. You can have a coffee in the café.
They can get the trolley and collect the goods. If they need to ask
someone where something is, they can ask an assistant. They will be
learning how to operate as an individual in a group, where no one
knows them.*

4   YOUR CHILDREN NEED TO REALISE THERE WILL BE NEW SKILLS TO LEARN IF THEY WANT TO DO WELL

Why? Some children continue to work at the same standard they did at primary school. They got top marks for the work at primary school and so they think the same level of work will bring them top marks again. Without realising it they are complacent. This complacency means they don't set a new standard for themselves. They might not get top marks for the work they are handing in. This can make them feel hostile and they can give up trying at all.

Try taking something your children are good at and asking them if they can remember what they thought was a good effort when they were five. Ask them what they do that is different now. See if they can tell you what they will need to do to make sure they are still good at it next year. This way they can see that anything they do can be improved and must be improved if they are to keep pace with their changing age.

Now you are on your own

There are many freedoms for secondary school pupils. Each age brings new freedoms encouraging children to look after themselves. Some children are so dependent on adults when they enter secondary school that they can't cope sensibly with the freedoms for their age. Teachers get to know them quickly but for all the wrong reasons. They are in danger of losing the respect of other children in their class. They are in danger of losing their self-esteem.

THE GIRL WHO DIDN'T KNOW HOW TO BE ELEVEN

Dawn was like a noisy bluebottle. She could never get on with her work because there was always something she thought she needed. Whenever Dawn didn't understand she put her hand up. If Dawn got stuck she would ask for help. If Dawn couldn't find her book she would tell the teacher. If Dawn hadn't heard what to do she would go and ask. If Dawn lost her pen she would ask her friends if she could borrow theirs. Dawn didn't realise that, if she was asking for help and assistance all the time, she wouldn't be doing any work. If she didn't do any work she wouldn't learn anything.

Dawn didn't understand what a pupil was. Neither did she understand the role of the teacher. She hadn't realised how important it was to listen to the teacher's explanations or instructions. Her parents had always told Dawn to ask when she didn't understand. Dawn hadn't understood that they meant she should listen first, then think about what she had heard and see if she could work it out. She should only ask if she didn't understand. While the teacher was talking, Dawn would fuss. As soon as everyone else began to work, Dawn's hand would shoot up because she hadn't heard what to do. When the teacher went to help her Dawn would say she was confused and didn't know where to start. Dawn thought she could get as much attention from her teacher as she could from her parents. Dawn was not able to work on her own at all. Dawn actually thought it was the teacher's job to make sure she did the work. She hadn't realised that she had a part to play in her own learning. She was convinced that she should have as much of the teacher's time as she needed. She felt she needed all the teacher's time. Dawn had to learn how to be part of a class of eleven-year-olds.

Children can only do well in their exams and tests if they have learnt how to get on with their work and do as much as they can on their own.

Dawn had been a bluebottle at primary school. Her

*behaviour hadn't been seen as a problem. Once she got to
secondary school she fell further and further behind.
Dawn didn't do very well in her exams because in exams
you have to work on your own and she couldn't. Although
Dawn was a bright child, she underachieved. The school
was providing good teaching but Dawn's serious
misunderstanding of her role as a pupil meant she missed
the benefits that were available to all.*

How to help your children get on and learn how to work by themselves

If you have children like Dawn it is easier to help them learn
to stand on their own feet in Year 7 than Year 11. In secondary
school standing on your own feet means:

- copying notes clearly so you have them for revision
- keeping a homework diary that is accurate and up to date
- getting homework in on time
- setting a goal so that the next piece of work is at least as good
  as the last and if possible better
- carrying the basic equipment suggested by the school

Not every child who is dependent is a bluebottle like Dawn.
Some are so silent they can be missed.

THE CHILD WHO MADE HERSELF INVISIBLE

*Yasmin had loved primary school. She was always helpful
and she nearly always got her work finished. She sat next
to a friend who knew what to do and if Yasmin was ever
stuck her friend would help her out. Sometimes Yasmin
would copy. Yasmin didn't do particularly well in her
tests but there were lots of people whose results were not as
good as hers.*

*When Yasmin went to secondary school she struggled.
Her friend had gone into another class and Yasmin had
no one to copy from. She didn't want the teacher to know*

*she couldn't do the work. She became very unhappy
because she felt lost and she was terrified she was stupid.
She never asked a question because she was worried that
she would not be able to understand the answer. Her
confidence drained away. She made herself as invisible as
possible.*

*Yasmin's parents knew she was unhappy but thought it
was because she was missing her friend. Yasmin was often
sick on the day there was a test but her parents didn't
know there was a test so they didn't realise there was a
connection. If Yasmin had homework she couldn't do, her
old friend from primary school would do it for her.*

*When it came to exams Yasmin did very badly. Doing
badly in the exams was just what she needed. Now
everyone knew she needed help.*

Be brave to benefit

Before Yasmin could benefit from any help she had to be
brave. She had to decide whether she wanted to be one of
life's winners. If she wanted to do well she had to be brave
enough to take help when she needed it. She had to be
brave enough to start again in some subjects because she had
missed so much learning when she had been letting her friend
do the work for her.

Yasmin began to really enjoy secondary school. She was no
longer afraid of making a mistake. She was prepared to put
her hand up to answer a question. She didn't panic if she got
the wrong answer. She would try again. She began to listen very
carefully to other people's answers because she realised she
could learn from her classmates as well as her teachers.

Mistakes happen and triers triumph

If you have children like Yasmin help them to understand that:

- ◆ a mistake is a chance to learn
- ◆ a mistake is a chance to be taught
- ◆ a mistake is a chance to discover a problem

Help your children know that if they try:

- they will get help
- they will get faster
- they will learn more
- they will stop falling behind
- they can catch up
- their exam results will get better

Move forward fearlessly

If your children can be brave:

- they will answer questions more often
- the teacher will notice them more often
- they will be able to look at the teacher and listen more carefully
- they will be ready to start work
- they will know what to do
- they will put more effort in
- they will achieve more each lesson

Who cares about me?

In primary school children get to know each other pretty well. Even if children feel they don't have friends, they do know a lot about all the people in their class. When children start secondary school they won't know people so well in the beginning. Some children will have friends from primary school and some children might have older brothers, sisters, cousins or friends who are looking out for them. Other children may not know anyone in their class or in the school.

The social challenges of secondary school are daunting for most children because many of them will have no experience of a large institution. Primary school teachers can keep a close watch on the children in their class. At secondary school there is much less continuous contact between teachers and pupils. In primary school, pupils move around with their teacher, from one part of the school to the other. In secondary school, when the lessons change, pupils get themselves from one class-room to the next. In primary school a teacher can sort out the social difficulties within a class. In secondary school sorting out those difficulties is not as easy. Some schools are better at it than others.

Who can I turn to?

In primary school your children's class teacher was mainly responsible for the children in her class. Primary teachers expect to talk to the children in their class and get to know them by working on lots of different areas with them. In secondary school, children have a form teacher, who will be friendly and supportive, but who will also be responsible for teaching hundreds of other children.

If children are to do well in secondary school they must become resilient. Children who are resilient are able to ignore little irritations and upsets. They are able to take strength from friends, home or teachers, to cope when things are difficult.

If children have had the chance to play with lots of people, in lots of situations, then they will be ready for the social challenge of being at secondary school. They will know how to deal with bossy people, silly people and aggressive people. They will have learnt how to recognise people they want to get to know better. They will have learnt ways of making friends. The more they have been allowed to sort out problems for themselves, with back-up when they need it, the more those skills will have developed. They will know that it doesn't always have to work for them all the time. They will know the role of an adult. An adult is there for guidance and direction. An adult is there to help you sort it out if you can't sort it out for yourself.

What do they think of me?

Starting at secondary school, children have a clean slate. The teachers build up impressions of children in the first few weeks as they notice how the children behave and work.

THE GIRL WHO THOUGHT SHE HAD
RUINED HER CHANCES AT SCHOOL . . .

Emma came charging through the front door on the second Monday after starting at secondary school. Her face was red and she looked as though her world had fallen apart. Her mum came into the hall to find Emma sitting on the stairs, sobbing. When Emma told her what had happened it sounded absolutely terrible. Teachers had been shouting at Emma. She was the worst person in the school and she could never go back. For a moment her mum started to panic. Through the sobs Emma's mum heard what had happened.

The whole class had been waiting outside the biology lab where some Year 10s had been doing experiments. The Year 7s had been looking through the windows at the Year 10s and the biology teacher had seen them. She was really cross and came out of the lesson to tell the class off. She had shouted at the whole class but because Emma had been standing at the front she felt the teacher thought it was all her fault. She was desperate. She had been determined to make a good impression at secondary school and now it had all gone wrong.

. . . AND HER MUM WHO KNEW
SHE HADN'T

Emma's mum told her to cheer up. She told her a story about when she had got into trouble in a new school. She had needed to go to the toilet. She had ended up in a place where other pupils were smoking. She knew it was silly to stay but she was desperate to go to the toilet. When she came out a teacher was waiting and all the pupils, including her, were sent to the headteacher. She had been terrified but the Head had understood and even the children who had been smoking were given another chance. She comforted Emma by explaining that everyone makes a mistake or gets into trouble occasionally. Even

*teachers. She told Emma it would all be forgotten about
and that if Emma did her best, that would be what was
remembered.*

Some children sail into secondary school. It seems to come at
just the right time for them to be able to use the skills they
have.

THE BOY WHO MADE A GOOD IMPRESSION

*Robert was one of those children every parent would love
to have. From the very first he knew he was a child and he
could learn from adults. He loved learning all the time.
He was proud each time he could do something new.*

- *When he was two he knew he could put his shoes on.*
- *When he was five he knew he could tie the laces.*
- *When he was six he could play out in the cul-de-sac.*
- *When he was eight he could walk to his friend's house.*
- *When he was ten he could get the shopping at the supermarket.*
- *At eleven he was safe in the science laboratory.*

*Robert recognised what a pupil was. He knew he was a
pupil and that he should make an effort to learn and
show the teacher that he was learning. In class he:*

- *listened to explanations and instructions*
- *did his best to put into practice what the teacher had said*

Teachers knew they could rely on Robert because:

- *when they looked at his work they would be seeing the result of
him doing his best*
- *when he was stuck, they would be able to judge how much
information he would need to get started again*
- *when they looked at his work and he had got the answer wrong
they could quickly check where the error had happened*

The rewards for Robert and his teachers included:

◆ the teachers knew that if Robert asked a question he would be ready to absorb the answer
◆ Robert could build on his learning all the time
◆ he found exams enjoyable
◆ Robert liked the chance to show what he knew
◆ Robert was interested in anything new
◆ Robert was not frightened about new information that was unexpected
◆ Robert was curious
◆ he was keen to add to his knowledge and understanding
◆ Robert understood that learning was a journey with no end

Children who can behave like Robert get the best teaching because they set up a situation where a teacher can do well.

Self-sufficiency in Year 7

Someone who is self-sufficient can look after their own belongings, know where they should be and know how to get there. If your children already take responsibility at home, they will have practised some of the skills they need in secondary school. This will help them to remember the right books and equipment, get to lessons on time and find their way around. They will be on the way to becoming self-sufficient pupils in a secondary school. To be self-sufficient, they will need to ask questions like:

WHERE AM I GOING?

When children in primary school leave their classroom to go to the hall, the playground or another room they are either shepherded by a teacher or in a small group. This contrasts sharply with the 'free for all' that many children think is happening when the bell goes for the end of a lesson at secondary school. The whole school gets up and begins to move. There is much less supervision in the corridors than in the primary school. Children are expected to follow rules to make sure everyone gets to their next class safely and on time.

Where do I belong?

In primary school children have a classroom base and a desk or place at a table that they feel is their own. When they go to secondary school they may have a classroom as a form room, but it is probably used by many other classes during the day.

Where are my belongings?

In secondary school children will have many belongings that they have to take care of. Some schools provide lockers but in many schools children have to carry their books, equipment and coats around with them. In primary school most children would only have to take care of outdoor clothes and a few belongings.

If your children are moving up to secondary school and you are concerned to make sure they will be independent you can help them.

1 Be firm. Remind yourself that if you don't make sure your children can be independent, their schoolwork will suffer. If schoolwork suffers so will exam results.
2 Explain how important it is to be self-sufficient.
3 Give them the chance to be self-sufficient.
4 Give them respect when they are self-sufficient. Children who have the chance to be self-sufficient at home are more likely to be self-sufficient at school. Looking after pets, mowing the lawn, putting out the empty milk bottles or the newspapers to be recycled are all chances to learn independence.
5 Remind your children to ask if there is something they don't understand about what you have given them to do.
6 If you can't motivate your children to be independent it may be that you are going too fast. You wouldn't expect an eleven-year-old to run a household, although some eleven-year-olds can. You do expect that a self-sufficient

eleven-year-old will help with housework, look after their own possessions, get to places they need to be on time and manage their pocket money.

7   If you can't motivate your children to co-operate with you, tell them what you are going to do if they don't shape up. This might be enough for them to get started. If you show your children that independence is important and you encourage them to become more independent they will realise how much respect you have for them.

8   If all else fails, you could have a sanction. You could deduct some pocket money, limit computer-time and TV time or stop a treat.

9   Your children will realise that, as they show more independence, everyone can 'chill out'.

Transition terrors

Any transition your children make will arouse a whole host of emotions. You will be proud that they have made it to this stage but you could be terrified when you think about what this might mean.

Don't panic. Your parents felt the same when you went to school. You know all the scrapes you got into or other people in the school were involved in, and you know you survived. Secondary schools are minefields but they are also pleasure domes. Don't dwell on the horrors. Most children will have highs as well as lows at school. Don't frighten your children with your own ghastly tales. There is a time and a place for everything.

Transition triumphs

Secondary schools welcome pupils who:

◆   are willing members of their community; children who are willing members of a community will be happy to follow the school rules, contribute to school life and make sure their behaviour outside the school brings credit to the school

- want to learn; children who want to learn are prepared to take guidance from the teacher, use the resources the school has to offer, contribute in discussion and work co-operatively with others in the school
- can look after their own belongings and take care of other people's possessions
- are individuals and enjoy school

10 tips for helping your children become impressive pupils

Impressive pupils know that they must pay attention. They know when to pay attention, where to pay attention and how to pay attention. If you want your children to develop their attention:

1 Don't jump in and try to solve all their problems. Allow them to answer for themselves.
2 Give them time to think.
3 Allow them to make decisions between different possibilities that you feel are sensible.
4 Explain why some choices they would like to make are not acceptable.
5 Have different responsibilities, bedtimes and amounts of pocket money so children can see that each age brings changes. Some things will be gained and some things will be lost.
6 Don't reward sloppy performance.
7 Praise attempts to learn a new skill.
8 Teach your children to speak clearly so that people will want to have a conversation with them.
9 Encourage your children to develop their conversational style – to be thoughtful and express their thoughts, use longer sentences, be able to ask questions and answer questions in a thoughtful way.

> **10** Encourage your children to make connections between new things they are hearing about and things they already have experience of. Sometimes you can help get the ball rolling by giving prompts.

Children who are successful know where to focus their attention. They know that they are separate from everyone around them. They know how to block distractions. They know how to be self-motivated. They know how to join in when necessary, even if it is momentary. They know their lives will be more interesting if they put something of themselves into every activity, whether it was something they wanted to do or not. They are reasonable, reasoning and autonomous.

COPING WITH REVISION, EXAMS AND RESULTS

CHAPTER 8

COPING WITH COURSEWORK

Coursework considerations

Coursework is compulsory. Children need to be able to think up ideas, try them out and write down what they have done. Coursework can cause conflict between parents and children and teachers and pupils. If an exam syllabus requires coursework then coursework has to be done. It has to be finished and handed in. Many children hate coursework. It seems to drag on and on. They are not sure if they are getting it right and they don't know how to organise themselves to do it.

Your children's projects may be used to decide which group they will be taught in. If they follow the suggestions for coursework when you are helping with projects, the finished piece of work will be a good reflection of your children's attitude and ability.

Coursework pitfalls to avoid

1 Trying to do it all at once.
2 Trying to do it at the last minute.
3 Trying to do it without discussing it with anyone.
4 Trying to get away with an excuse for why they haven't done it well, on time or at all.
5 Not understanding that the teachers must follow the rules for coursework in the same way all pupils have to.
6 Thinking other people aren't doing it either.

7 Not realising that by the time coursework is part of their exam, they are expected to use their 'free' time to do it.
8 Thinking they can copy someone else's.
9 Thinking it doesn't really matter because it is only worth a few marks.
10 Wasting time being angry because they have to do it.

How to avoid the pitfalls

MAKE SURE THEY DON'T LOSE THEIR WORK

◆ Most people don't have a space that they are sure will be undisturbed. It is important to make sure that coursework is always tidied away so your children can get started whenever they have time.

◆ It is helpful if your children file all their pieces of paper in separate plastic wallets, so that they can easily see what they have done.

◆ File scrappy notes as well as completed notes until they are sure that they have used all the information on each piece of paper. If they haven't the time to file, they can keep the pieces of paper they have been working on inside their folder or in a box marked 'coursework'.

COLLECT USEFUL INFORMATION

If they see articles about their coursework, thay can cut them out or photocopy them and put them in the box as well so they can use them when they have the time. Make sure they note on each cutting the date and the name of the magazine or newspaper it came from.

PROTECTING THEIR WORK

Encourage your children to:

◆ Decide what they need to carry with them all the time and only take what is necessary.

◆ Make sure when they are carrying coursework that it is

protected. Large plastic wallets with zippers offer efficient protection.

- Write their name on everything they carry, so it can be returned should it be mislaid.
- Keep a copy of each piece of coursework and avoid taking it away from home. Date it and, if they have done several redrafts, number each one.

ORGANISING THEIR WORK

- As they finish with each piece of paper, they can put it in a folder and store the folder somewhere, just in case they need the material again.
- They can decide what they need to do away from home or school to complete the project. It could be interviews, sketches, videos, visits to theatres, museums or galleries or special venues associated with a particular piece of coursework. They can work out how they are going to get there, the cost, how much time to set aside, and if one trip will be enough.
- If they are doing an interview, they can ask if the conversation can be taped, but check before the interview that the equipment is working.

How to get a good mark

The examiners will be looking for evidence of students' ability to:

- follow directions precisely
- show individual flair within set limits
- deal with a task in a time limit
- deal with all aspects of the task fully
- communicate an understanding of the instructions
- use the basic skills that the coursework needs
- use additional material or skills to enhance the quality of coursework

The assignment is always the solution to a problem. A good assignment will show how your children have identified the areas that need addressing, found ways to address them and demonstrated their results.

Coursework requires careful organisation and an ability to deal with several parts of the project in parallel. Your children might follow one line of enquiry and then need to leave it while they follow another.

They will be judged on their ability to keep to the point, write clearly and keep their work logical so that someone can follow the way they have seen the problem.

Making sure they are pleased with their coursework

Your children need to give enough time to:

- do it thoughtfully
- draft and redraft
- check the quality of the presentation
- reflect on what has been written
- review the work before handing it in for the teacher to look at, prior to discussing it together
- reflect on the discussion with the teacher
- make amendments or even start again if the work has missed the point
- research
- explore possibilities

Writing an essay or a story that gets good marks

Whether your children are writing a story or an essay, they will use the same skills. To get a high mark in an essay or a story they need to:

- make sure they know what they are writing about
- have a beginning, middle and end
- remember all the time what it is they are writing about and keep to the point
- remember someone will read what they have written. The

reader will want to feel interested, so the writing must have life. Writing has life when the writer puts in something of themselves
- ◆ make sure that what they write makes sense; the people reading it will have to understand it
- ◆ use punctuation, correct grammar, correct spellings and good sentences

Be a story writer

If your children are writing fiction they need to:

- ◆ think about the ideas they are going to explore. Try to be original
- ◆ think and write about what the characters would see, hear, touch, smell and taste in the world they have created
- ◆ think and write about how the characters would react to each other and the things that happen to them
- ◆ learn the rules for writing speech
- ◆ use a thesaurus to enrich the language
- ◆ remember that the narrative tells the story; it gives an outline of what happens
- ◆ the descriptions add colour to the story; they help the reader feel they are part of the event
- ◆ use the dialogue to tell people what is happening
- ◆ look at writing they like and try to work out what makes them want to read it
- ◆ take opportunities to read good literature; good literature gives them the chance to experience the world through other people's lives; even a paragraph from good literature will give them the benefit of rich language, carefully crafted sentences and clear thoughts; your children will feel the joy that comes from being invited into the world of other people. They too are writing down their thoughts

Explore a subject from all angles

Factual essays that need your children to discuss, compare and analyse will mean your children have to draw on their own knowledge. People who do well in these essays read widely. Newspapers are a good source of articles. Your children can compare articles to see how one topic has been written about differently. If they limit their study to the work given them by their teacher, or what is in a textbook, they may pass but won't get a good mark. If they only talk about their experience and don't refer to anything learnt at school, they may write a wonderful essay, but fail. If they can link their wider understanding to the work they have done at school and write what they know and answer the question, they will do well.

The secret of success in writing something that will get high marks is the knowledge that everyone they are writing about is human. Human beings are capable of different courses of action at any point and that is the fascination for the reader.

◆ If your children are writing a piece of fiction, the reader will follow the possibilities they have created.

◆ If they are writing a factual report on something that happened, the reader will want to know what the human aspects were, such as: How were people involved? What did they do? What choices did they make? What affects the characters?

◆ If they are writing an opinion piece, the reader will want to know how they reacted to the choices others made.

CHAPTER 9

REVISION

How to make revision successful

Remember that children will need time and care if they are going to study well. They will need time to work, time to rest and time to play.

What parents can do

You will need to help your children organise their time until they can organise it themselves. Organise family time around study time. It is important to remember that exams are only a part of life. Keep a sense of balance for the whole family. Younger children will be influenced by what they see. If they are learning how to stay calm in the run-up to exams they will have a balanced attitude when they do exams as well.

What children can do

Children can save themselves time and stress if they sort out their space when they are revising.

Children can make sure they have a relaxed working environment

- ◆ Organise working space.
- ◆ Make sure there is air in the room.
- ◆ Wear comfortable clothes.
- ◆ Sit in different places.
- ◆ Put unnecessary items into a box.
- ◆ When it's time for a break, tidy the working space.

- Sit on a comfortable chair that gives good support.
- Make a space where they feel in control.
- Keep revision notes in some sort of order.
- Have some sharp pencils, a sharpener, a rubber, a ruler, a favourite pen and some tissues nearby.

Expanding children's minds – increasing their marks

THEY CAN GET 'A'S WHEN THEY GIVE MORE

- They can read more than just the set books.
- A good general knowledge will sometimes be enough for some exam or test questions. They can cut out and read articles that apply to the subject.
- Check radio and television programmes. They can record programmes to do with their subject.
- General knowledge is always a great asset.
- If they can't do something it is probably because they didn't understand the section before. They need to look back in their notes.

They need to:

- learn how to skim-read
- learn how to scan through a piece of writing to find out facts
- use libraries
- use encyclopedias
- read around the subject

Profit from planning

SOMETIMES PEOPLE THINK THAT STUDY IS ALL ABOUT MEMORY. SUCCESSFUL STUDY IS MORE TO DO WITH PLANNING

Your children need to:

- make a timetable
- be prepared for something to take longer than expected
- do a little and often

- find out what is needed to get an A and see if they can study in the right way to get it
- practise writing neatly
- spend ten minutes thinking – it can save hours of revising
- make sure they have the equipment they need
- make lists
- find out what other people want in the day so that they can fit in
- let people know how long they are going to study so they can be left in peace
- make a plan for each session
- have a checklist to see if the plan worked
- revise in small chunks

Getting down to it

LOTS OF PEOPLE WASTE TIME BECAUSE THEY DON'T WANT TO START TO WORK

They can:

- set a question and see if they can answer it
- tell someone else about what they have been revising
- see how much they can write in five minutes
- practise writing answers in a set time
- get started
- accept that a lot of study is slog
- start studying with something they can do rather than something they can't
- write down any resentments they have and then get on with their work
- whenever they don't follow their timetable they must not give up – they can adjust the timetable and get going again

Fitness fights fatigue

STUDY IS NOT A SOLITARY SENTENCE. YOUR CHILDREN NEED TO KNOW THAT PEOPLE CARE ABOUT THEM AND THEY NEED TO CARE ABOUT THEMSELVES

They can:

◆ have breaks
◆ exercise
◆ leave something that is too hard and do something else before coming back to try again
◆ relax
◆ eat sensibly
◆ practise being calm
◆ practise drawing and labelling diagrams
◆ have a stretch by an open window, door or outside if they are feeling stale
◆ rest their eyes
◆ use hand exercises to keep hands and fingers flexible
◆ set a time for coming back after a break
◆ have rests during the day
◆ keep an interest in their hobbies
◆ use a timer
◆ get up and go for a walk if their mind is wandering
◆ use a relaxation exercise to help focus
◆ try to drink as much water as possible
◆ avoid working in a stuffy room
◆ do some breathing exercises
◆ have enough sleep

Your children need to stop and check

THEY SHOULD CHECK WHETHER THEY ARE TAKING IN WHAT THEY ARE STUDYING. STARING AT THE BOOK IS NOT NECESSARILY LEARNING

They can:

- write down the definitions
- use a dictionary
- make notes
- use keywords
- write down as many words as they can think of to do with the topic they are revising
- check they know how to spell the keywords
- make a glossary – a good way of revising
- write out a definition and then check the dictionary if they think they know what a word means
- if they are stuck always write what they know before they check to find out what they should know
- make up diagrams to help them remember
- underline any new thing they have learnt
- list things that have similarities when they are revising
- separate out facts so they will be able to use those facts in lots of different places
- make up mnemonics to help them remember
- make up acrostics for key points
- practise something they have revised
- do the exercises – not just read them through
- see how many questions their answer can fit
- see how many ways they can answer the question

Be realistic

IF YOUR CHILDREN LOOK AT WAYS THEY CAN STUDY AND TRY THEM OUT THEY WILL SUCCEED. IF THEY LOOK AT REASONS WHY THEY CAN'T STUDY THEIR RESULTS MIGHT BE DISAPPOINTING

Encourage your children to:

◆ make links between subjects
◆ remember that going back helps them go forward
◆ remember that everything is connected to something
◆ avoid bluffing
◆ recognise their weaknesses so they can turn them into strengths
◆ recognise their strengths and make sure they don't become their weaknesses
◆ learn from their mistakes
◆ be precise when they can
◆ look at the work of someone who has got an A if they are aiming for an A
◆ make sure they fill in any gaps in their notes when they have been away or off sick
◆ revise from the best notes possible
◆ make some new notes if their notes from class are not good
◆ avoid blaming themselves or the teacher if they have done badly on something
◆ ignore people who look as though they are not working
◆ make sure study is a commitment
◆ tell their friends how much time they can spend with them and then go even if there is a crisis
◆ tell the family how much time they have got to help and then stop when the time is up
◆ keep in their mind their commitment to study no matter what else they are doing
◆ not give up
◆ remember that if they don't do anything, nothing gets done
◆ avoid looking for reasons why they can't do any work
◆ do a little bit of work because it is better than doing none at all

Don't waste time worrying

YOUR CHILDREN MAY WORRY WHEN THEY ARE WORKING THAT
THEY ARE NEVER GOING TO BE GOOD ENOUGH. MOST PEOPLE
FEEL ANXIOUS, AT SOME POINT, THAT EXAMS WILL SHOW
THEM UP

Your children will feel calmer if they:

- only think about their study when they are studying
- take a break when they are feeling anxious and look up some
  key words, remember to be relaxed or copy a helpful passage
  or paragraph
- keep their final goal in mind
- don't compare themselves with anyone else
- remember that everyone learns differently
- find their way of learning because then they will learn
  successfully

Give themselves a pat on the back

IF YOUR CHILDREN ARE WORKING THEY WILL BE IMPROVING.
PEOPLE WHO LEARN WELL NOTICE THEIR LITTLE SUCCESSES

- The more effort they put in, the greater their chance of
  succeeding.
- Your children will learn well if they notice all their success.

Maximise memory

MUCH OF THE WORK YOUR CHILDREN HAVE TO DO FOR AN EXAM
WILL INVOLVE USING THEIR MEMORY

They can:

- write out a list of facts from the textbook that they think
  should be in the answer
- see how many things on the list they can write down when
  they are not looking at the list

- prepare some opening sentences for essays
- put up facts they have to remember around the house
- read notes on to a tape and play it back
- check the dictionary for words they don't know
- make a note of what unusual words mean
- before doing a maths exercise check a worked example
- put up tips around the house where they can see them
- say things out loud
- take notes
- decide when they study best and plan their day around that
- use scrap paper to jot down ideas

Look around

TENSION CAN GET IN THE WAY. WHEN YOUR CHILDREN ARE
FEELING TENSE ENCOURAGE THEM TO REMEMBER THAT THEY ARE
NOT ALONE

They can:

- use friends to bounce ideas off
- see their family as their friends
- stretch often
- remember their parents are on their side
- take responsibility for their own work and parents won't have to nag
- think about how much energy and time they have. They may have to give something up to get the results they want

CHAPTER 10

PREPARING FOR EXAMS

Making the most of time before an exam

If three weeks, three days, three hours or three minutes before the exam, your children think they don't know enough to pass, this is what they could do . . .

◆ If it is three weeks before the exam, they do have a chance of learning enough to do well in a couple of questions. If they choose carefully they may be lucky enough for those questions to come up.

◆ If it is three days before the exam, they can revise something that is close to a topic they think they know quite well. They can look through their books and make links between one area and another.

◆ If it is three hours before the exam they can revise something that they do know so that they will get the best mark possible, if they are lucky enough for that topic to come up.

◆ If it is three minutes before the exam and they haven't realised until now that they don't know enough, they are probably just panicking. They need to relax. They can concentrate on one of their senses. If they are standing or sitting they can notice the weight of their body as it presses down on the floor or the chair. They could choose to notice the sounds that are around them, including ones nearby and ones in the distance. The important thing is to become calm and then stay calm; this exercise will help them do that.

Shift the focus

The temptation before your children take a test or exam can be to try to encourage them to just get on with the revision. This can work for many children but not for children who are in a panic. You will need to try to shift the focus. By shifting the focus on to a different activity unrelated to the test or exam, you will remind your children that there is more to their world than this exam that has gripped them with fear. If your children are fraught, suggest that they:

- have a bath
- go for a walk
- help get tea ready
- read a book
- do a relaxation exercise

If you can give your children the feeling that it is all right to think about something else for a while, they will begin to calm down. They will get the sense that they can control at least part of their lives. Remind them that there are many things they can do and do well. They will be able to do their best in the exam and find out whether their revision has been successful.

I'M GOING TO FAIL AND IT'S ALL SOMEONE ELSE'S FAULT

Sarah came home in a terrible mood. She snarled at her brother, was rude to her mother, stomped into the kitchen and started raiding the fridge. Finally, after having been nasty to everyone she complained that she had a test the next day. It was on all the French they had done in the last month and she knew she was going to fail. She said she was going to fail because the children in her class always talked so she couldn't hear the teacher. Her normal teacher had been off and the stand-in teacher was no good. Some people in the class were better than she was

*because they had parents who could help. Everyone else in
the class thought the same way Sarah did and she was fed
up. Once she'd finished complaining, arguing and being
generally unpleasant she went into her bedroom and
turned her music up very loud.*

Principles of successful parenting when faced with your children's fear of failure

When children get into a state like this the last thing they need
is for you to be as angry with them as they are with the rest of
the world. When children throw wobblies they have lost their
grip. They are creating a situation that is as out of control as
they feel themselves.

1 Don't get sucked in to responding to every complaint. You
   are aiming to reduce the fear. You are not going to sort out
   every complaint. You are going to show your children how to
   deal with panic.
2 Let your children know that you will help with their revision.
   Encourage them to get on with what needs to be done. Help
   them calm down.
3 Remind them of activities that they find relaxing. Everyone
   needs to recognise that this time for relaxation is essential
   before revision can begin again.
4 Be available if your help is needed but remember your aim is
   to develop effective, independent learning in your children.

Children can hate exams because they think they are going to fail

This sense of doom may bear no relation at all to the work they
have done, the success they have had in the past or how other
people see them. They just feel that they are not going to be
good enough and they can't bear that feeling.

Suggestions for your children to help prevent failure

1 *Read more than is in the textbook.* This gives you another way of looking at the same subject. Read different explanations of the same topic. This will introduce you to different vocabulary for the subject and increase your understanding of the topic. You also get an idea of how this topic might be linked to other topics. Key words and key ideas will come up repeatedly in your reading.

2 *Eat.* Make sure you have eaten something sensible either before you start work or before the exam. If you get hungry you find your brain will lose interest in anything else other than food.

3 *Sleep.* You can get away with not having enough sleep occasionally but you can't keep going efficiently when you are tired. It is a good idea to develop a pattern of sleep for exam times.

4 *Exercise.* If you exercise you are getting oxygen into your system. This will help you work better.

5 *Beware of kidding yourself.* It is important to write down just what is going to be tested so you don't persuade yourself that you either have to do too much or can get away with doing too little.

6 *Relax.* Relaxation is a way of disciplining your mind. Disciplining your mind is a powerful way of preventing panic. Go for a walk, look at the view or listen to a piece of music. You will discover the best way to clear your mind.

Success in exams and tests comes from confidence and knowledge

Many parents feel that if their children can learn the techniques for staying calm, then their results will improve. *Beware.* People who are sitting exams have to know the information or skills that are being tested. All the confidence in the world won't inspire them to solve a simultaneous equation if they don't know how to do it.

Sometimes children who have done well in a test decide that they don't need to work quite so hard. Don't panic. It is only when their next results are disappointing that they realise why studying matters. Many adults find the memory of sitting in an exam room with no idea what to do remains one of their most embarrassing moments. They use it as a warning to themselves whenever they think a challenge will be easy.

Parents can have given children their support, children can have prepared properly, but no one can predict every eventuality.

Prepare for the unexpected during an exam

Unexpected things can happen in exams. Exams aren't only about the information you know. Success can depend on being able to cope with the unexpected while still doing the exam.

THE GIRL WHO COULD COPE WITH ANYTHING

Amy's mother and father had prepared her beautifully for her first year exams. She had revised steadily, combined study and leisure very well, got into a very good sleep pattern so she woke each morning refreshed and was eating sensible food designed to give her the best chance mentally and physically. Everyone was pleased with the preparation.

When Amy lined up to go into the hall for the exam she

was surprised to see that pupils from another year were lining up as well. The teachers had decided that a good way of making sure no one was cheating was to have children from different years sitting next to each other. All the Year 7 girls would sit by Year 9 boys and Year 9 girls next to Year 7 boys. The children sat down and Amy found herself sitting next to the Year 9 'Casanova'. She could barely breathe with the excitement and kept trying to catch her friends' eyes. She also began to giggle. All her careful preparation counted for nothing. She was so excited and felt so important and incredibly lucky. She did manage to get started on the exam at the right time but only a tiny part of her attention was devoted to answering the questions.

When everyone filed out of the exam all the Year 7 girls clustered about her asking what it had been like and she felt as if she must have already come top. When the marks were given out she was relieved to discover that she had done very well. She had been worried because whenever she thought about that exam she knew that a lot of her mind had been imagining becoming Casanova's girlfriend. Because Amy was well prepared for the exam this hiccup didn't affect her performance. Children need to know that if they are well prepared unexpected things won't mean that they get bad marks.

Practical advice to give your children before an exam or test

THE DAY BEFORE

Ask your children to collect all the equipment they are going to need for their exam and put it out so it can be checked. Think about what needs to be done for the next day and see what you can get organised ahead of time. Ask if there is anything your children might need you to sort out: food treats, uniform, tissues, new socks, ink cartridges, a battery for the calculator, a new watchstrap.

Part of the problem on the day of the test or exam is that you are as nervous or possibly even more nervous than your children. If you sort out your own stress, you will be able to help them sort out theirs.

If you can, wake up before they do. Stretch, have a glass of water and do some relaxation. When your children emerge, smile and look welcoming. If you have time, set the table for breakfast so your children have a chance to settle while they eat.

Try to make some time for them to get anything off their chest. Their minds will be clearer for the rest of the day. Reassure them that you know that they are hoping for a good result. Remind them of something you know they can do well now since they have done some revision.

Encourage them to get enough food to keep them going.

Ask them what they plan to do when they get to school. If you have time, ask them if they would like to do a relaxation exercise with you.

Many teachers suggest that when children go to school on the day of the exam they:

- ◆ avoid people who panic
- ◆ make sure they are wearing a watch
- ◆ wait in a place where people are calm
- ◆ take something to suck that doesn't make a noise
- ◆ take a drink if this is allowed
- ◆ go to the toilet before the exam
- ◆ have a few notes to read
- ◆ take a coin for the phone to make contact with home
- ◆ take some tissues
- ◆ wish other people luck
- ◆ remind themselves that they can do it
- ◆ think of other times when they have passed exams

Once your children are in the exam room suggest that they:

◆ make sure the table doesn't wobble. A small piece of card put under the table leg will make sure it stays still while they write. The teacher in charge of the exam or the invigilator will help your children to sort it out
◆ take some deep breaths while they wait for the exam to begin
◆ get comfortable
◆ try not to get distracted by anyone else
◆ focus when they fill in their details

When they open the paper they need to:

◆ read the question carefully. It is important they sort out what is information to get them on track and what is the instruction the examiner wants them to follow.
◆ highlight or underline key words in the question.
◆ remember that their answers have to be understood by the examiner so they must write their answers clearly

CHAPTER 11

AFTER THE EXAMS – DEALING WITH RESULTS

Ask your children how the exam went

- When Karina did an exam her parents would ask her how it had gone. Karina and her parents would sit and chat through what she could remember of the paper. She would touch on the bits she found easy, those she had to think about and the bits she thought were difficult.
- When Peter did an exam his parents would ask him how it had gone. He would say it had been okay. He would smile disarmingly but wouldn't volunteer any more information.
- When John did an exam his parents would ask him how it had gone. John would be very confident and always assure them that the exam had been hard but he was sure he had done well.
- When Emma did an exam her parents would ask her how it had gone. She would happily chat about how nervous she had felt, what other pupils had said about the exam, dramas that had happened and how many mints she had eaten in the course of the paper.
- When Daniel did an exam his parents would ask how it had gone. Daniel would always say that he hadn't been able to do the paper, neither had any of his friends, and it was all the teacher's fault.
- When Richard did an exam his parents would ask how it had gone. He was always very shaky and convinced he had failed.

He was very hard on himself and would blame himself for not knowing enough, not being clever enough and not having studied hard enough.

If you want your children to be like Karina, and life can be easier for everyone if they are, then you have to do what her parents did. They taught Karina that the important thing was not to criticise anyone, especially herself. Instead they taught her how to think about her work. She learnt to:

- ◆ recognise what she had done well
- ◆ compare her most recent effort against previous efforts
- ◆ notice improvement, no matter how small
- ◆ spot any weak areas and work out how she could improve them
- ◆ think about whether she had put enough effort in
- ◆ check whether the things she found difficult were because she didn't know enough or she wasn't fast enough

Karina's parents had seen how damaging it could be for a child to think that if something was wrong then it had to be somebody's fault. They wanted to make sure their children would learn that anything they did could be thought about. If they thought about it they could decide how to improve it.

Exams matter but there is always tomorrow

A test or exam rarely shuts or opens a door forever. We all have many chances to show others what we know. Failing an exam can help us learn. We learn how to:

- ◆ plan
- ◆ set aside time to prepare
- ◆ organise our time to fit in study

- decide what we really want
- do more work than is set in order to increase our chances of success because we give ourselves a cushion against the unexpected

What do I say if my children get low marks for a test?

SOME THINGS YOU CAN ASK . . . .

- Do they know why?
- What was the highest and what was the lowest mark?
- Do they know what they got wrong?
- Would it help if you had a chat to their teacher?
- Do they think a tutor would help?

SOME THINGS YOU CAN SAY . . .

- That test is over now, we can start to work for the next test and improve on the mark.

SOME THINGS YOU CAN DO . . .

- If the test paper has been brought home you could give them practice on the questions they had problems with and see if it was just nerves or a misunderstanding, rather than not knowing how to do them.
- Go for a walk.
- Kick a football.
- Go window shopping.

SOME THINGS TO AVOID . . .

Try not to:

- expect perfection from yourself or your children
- scream, sulk, say something nasty, sob

- ring a friend to whinge so your child can hear
- threaten, throw things
- refuse to speak, refuse to listen, refuse to cook tea
- ground your child for a fortnight, grab him by the arm and shake him, grind your teeth
- send back the bike, stop his pocket money, slam the door
- disconnect his computer, take the plug off his television or confiscate his sound system

Of course, you will not manage to behave like an adult person every time test results are disappointing. You are only human, like the rest of us, and we all behave badly more often than we think we should.

We only have to read the papers to see how often people behave badly and we know even in our everyday life that few of us behave perfectly all the time. Sometimes parents believe their children have the right to perfect parents and they put terrible pressure on themselves. Some parents believe anything they decide is right because they never question their parenting. When this happens children can suffer terrible pressure whenever they don't meet their parents' picture of perfection. Parenting is always difficult because the demands are constant and constantly changing. Sometimes parents feel inadequate or guilty because of other demands that are made on their time, energy, attention or patience. *Do not panic.* If you remember that you might need to make up that time in the future, if one of your children is struggling then your children will not be affected badly by the natural ups and downs of family life.

HELPING YOUR CHILDREN LEARN BASIC SKILLS

CHAPTER 12

UNDERSTANDING HOW TO LEARN MOST EFFECTIVELY

Learning styles

What is learning? Learning is when you allow something going on around you to change you. How do you learn? You might be listening to a teacher, thinking about what she is saying and rearranging what you know to take in the new information. You could be looking at a view and working out how what you see fits in with what you expect to see. Learning is:

◆ noticing the unexpected
◆ recognising similarities, making links between what was known and what you can now see
◆ taking in new information and rearranging the old to get the best fit
◆ working out which things you need to select to remember
◆ working out which things you misunderstood

Learning does not happen by magic. There will be lots of things that we can't remember learning. Even if we can't remember how we learnt, there will still have been a time when we were taught. There was a change in us from ignorance to knowledge. We learn some things very easily. Other things take us a long time to learn and occasionally we realise we know and can do something that we never remember having been taught. To pass exams and tests we have to show what we have learnt. Marks are awarded when we show evidence that we have learnt something. The better the evidence, the better the mark.

How children learn

Learning happens in three ways:

1 *You can learn incidentally.* This means when you watch programmes on television, listen to other people's conversations or ask some questions, you build up knowledge without actually trying to learn anything. Younger children in the family often learn like this. They hear someone else doing their homework, watch somebody else colour in, or get included in a game with other people who can play. No one expects them to be any good at any of these things because they are younger, but suddenly they show they know what to do. They have been learning even though no one knew they were being taught.
2 *You can learn incrementally.* This means you learn little by little, usually when you are being taught in some way or other. This is the sort of learning that happens when you are learning basic skills. Students will need to learn some basic skills or knowledge every time they start a new topic. Success in exams comes from understanding that basic skills are essential and take time to learn.
3 *You can learn intuitively.* This means you suddenly understand how to do something because you have put together different things you know and made a giant leap in understanding.

Using all methods of learning

Some children get stuck in thinking that only one way of learning is possible or acceptable.

◆ If they think intuitive learning is the only way they can learn,

they won't have any idea how much they can learn if they
listen or they keep trying.

- ◆ If they think incremental learning is the only way, they may
  only learn when they decide something is important.
  Children like this don't use school trips or previous
  knowledge as a way of moving forward. They will work hard
  from a book or in class but they could do better if they
  realised the power of their intuition and the power of
  making connections.
- ◆ Children who think they can only learn incidentally are often
  good in a group, love doing experiments, will answer all sorts
  of questions, but can't get on with their work on their own.

For children to get top marks they have to learn to use each
form of learning.

Ideas to encourage children to use all the learning styles

INCIDENTAL LEARNING

- ◆ Draw a circle on a piece of paper and think what it could
  be. This can be done with two or more people. Try to
  get 100 possibilities. If you get stuck, look around you, in
  the kitchen or in the bathroom. What circular object
  from the house could it be? Think of foods. Think of
  games. You will get lots of ideas. More importantly, you
  will be encouraging your children to learn from what is
  around them and to notice the store of information they
  already have in their heads.
- ◆ Get your children to use a reading book to find as many
  different ways of saying 'said' as they can. Words like
  'shouted', 'whispered' and 'asked' could go on the list
  and you may find ones like 'muttered', 'grunted' and
  'spat'. Your children will be surprised at how many

---

words there are. It is a good idea for them to look in several books. You will be showing your children that they can learn from all sorts of activities. They don't have to wait for a lesson or when they are doing their homework. They realise that learning can be fun.

INCREMENTAL LEARNING

◆ Some children will learn spelling lists incrementally. All children should learn the words on the spelling list so that they will be able to use them when they speak or write. Many children have to write sentences using the words in their lists. You can teach them how to increase their knowledge of the way a word can be used by playing a game called Building A Sentence.

Take the first word from the list – *Egyptians*. The second person thinks of a word and puts it in front – *The Egyptians*. The next person adds a word at the end – *The Egyptians lived*. The next person can finish the sentence – *The Egyptians lived on the Nile*. The next person may have a go at improving the sentence – **The ancient Egyptians lived on the Nile and were farmers**. In this way you are building your children's knowledge of how the word can be used and information about when the word can be used. This is a game for two or more people. You will have taught your children a way of using what they know as building blocks.

INTUITIVE LEARNING

◆ Put a collection of items into a bag. One at a time, the people playing put their hand into the bag. They grasp one of the items but don't bring it out. Using their sense of touch they describe what they have in their hand but never name it, e.g. 'It is plastic, it has a lot of spiky bits, it is as long as my hand, it feels quite light, I can close my

> hand around it.' See if the other people playing can work out what it is (a comb). If they can't they can ask the person describing the object some questions to try to get more information. Children will be learning that they can use their senses to make sense. They can have a guess, see if they are right and if not, think again.

Learning is many things. It goes through many stages. Children may think they are learning:

◆ if somebody is telling them what to do
◆ by going to school
◆ when they come top
◆ when they finish their work first
◆ if they spend a lot of time doing their work
◆ when they can 'parrot' something back to you without understanding it

Children may not know that the ultimate goal of learning is to be able to do it on their own.

Learning how to work on your own

Provided children are building towards being able to work on their own, they are learning. Exams catch out children who don't realise that the ultimate goal of learning is to be able to do it on their own. They may have been successful when they were doing their homework, they may have spent time reading through their notes, but they haven't checked how much they can do without help. When they get into the exam they find that what they can do alone is less than they could do when they were at home. They can then believe that they are all right at everything except exams.

Warning! Sometimes disappointing results have more to do with not being able to do the work than with a lack of confidence, lack of sleep, headache or the temperature in the room.

Check what you think they know

Sometimes it is so confusing when children can't learn something that you really are stumped. If you focus on each thing your children are doing, you will be able to see their logic. When you see their logic, you will see where the fault is in their logic.

Each time you are going to help your children, think about what you are assuming they know. Check, as you are working, whether the mistakes that are being made are because of the new work or because of a problem they have from something they learnt in the past.

Clarity and structure

No matter what your children's learning style, they must aim for clarity. Even if they can't understand what to do, they can make your job much easier. If they are clear you can then tell what they:

- ◆ know
- ◆ only half know
- ◆ have no idea about at all

You can help your children become clear by getting them to give you instructions clearly. 'This is my spelling homework. You have to test me to see which words I already know. I have to learn the ones I don't know and then you have to test me on all the ones on the list and I have to get them all right before I can finish.'

If children give messages to other people clearly they are practising clarity of thought. They see how quickly a job can be done or a message can be understood when they give information in the right order.

Clarity, when doing a piece of work, means that each stage has a structure and each structure must be clear.

Your children will be expected to write the date and the title of their work each time an exercise book is used at school. This is done to provide a clear reference for teachers or for themselves. If they are revising later they will be reminded of the time they did the work. They will be learning how to organise their work. Each time they write the date and heading their minds will begin to focus on the task. If you are planning some holiday work to do at home it is a good idea to start each session by writing the date and heading to give some clarity and structure to the work that is to follow.

Children who are successful understand how they can learn efficiently. They are able to pick out from what they have done what was successful. They are able to show what they have done so that other people can see their success.

CHAPTER 13

ENCOURAGING SUCCESSFUL READING

Success in reading brings success in exams

All exams involve reading. Many tests depend on reading as well. Successful readers probably:

- read newspapers
- use a dictionary if they don't know a word
- read reviews of sporting events, films, books, computer games
- belong to a library
- play word games
- use encyclopedias
- buy books
- borrow books
- receive books as presents
- ask for book tokens
- use an atlas
- use books to learn more about their hobbies or interests
- have books around (the toilet is a good place to keep a store of books, as is the car)
- read while they are waiting
- remember which author they like
- are able to say why they like particular books
- want to talk to others about the books they have read
- will have at least one book on the go
- probably see other people reading for enjoyment

What you can do to make sure your children become successful readers

To help your children learn to read you need to:

◆ develop awareness and patience
◆ explore books with your children
◆ explore words with your children

When reading with your children patience is essential. Reading can be a peaceful activity if you are patient. By using a flexible and friendly approach you will be teaching your children how to love learning and how to love reading. Your children don't have to say every word on the page. Reading with your children need not be a punishment that must be endured.

Read all the time

Just think about what you have read today. Quite apart from this book that you are reading for information, you may have read road signs, recipes, a letter from the bank, a school report or some junk mail. So, what is reading and how did you manage to do it?

To read words you have to understand that the letters that make up words are a code. In each word the letters are put together in a particular way. When you learnt to read you learnt how to identify sounds in speech and how to link those sounds to particular letters. Children who are happy with learning to read are children who are happy to experiment with different sounds. The same letters do not always make the same sound. The same sound does not always come from the same letters.

Tips for reading with your children

Reading aloud is important. When your children read aloud you can find out where mistakes are happening. Are they:

◆ leaving off the ends of words?
◆ putting the last letter at the front of the word?
◆ saying an 'a' where they should be saying an 'e'?
◆ putting in their own words?
◆ letting their minds wander?
◆ having trouble keeping their place?

Be patient

None of these problems is catastrophic. They don't have to be sorted out in one evening. Some problems even seem to sort themselves out.

Go at your own pace. As your children get more confident their pace will increase. You will be making progress. Your children will have a go even when they are unsure. They will try to work the answers out for themselves and if that is beyond them, will come to you for guidance.

Correct your children gently. If you can guide them towards the answer rather than give them the answer you will build up their ability to learn. Their ability to learn will grow when they find ways of working out the answers for themselves.

The reason parents are asked to read with their children is so that there is more than one adult keeping an eye on what is happening. Teachers will be delighted if you can encourage your children to enjoy books.

The early reader

If your children are reading books that are mainly pictures, you can make reading fun by:

◆ talking with them about the pictures
◆ reading the story to them

- looking together for all the names in the story
- finding all the three-, four- or five-letter words in the story
- thinking of different endings for the story

Opening up reading

Parents and teachers of successful readers encourage children by opening books. They open books to read themselves, to read to their children, to find information in response to their children's questions. They provide books from the library, as presents, from jumble sales or from second-hand bookshops. They read newspapers. They buy magazines. They present information that will stimulate their children to think about current affairs including politics, sport, fashion, music, technology and the environment.

Encouraging wide reading

Parents of successful readers will find ways of encouraging their children to read more widely or adventurously.

Parents of good readers will understand that sometimes all readers will spend time reading lightweight or trivial material. Reading is a personal experience and children are very sensitive if their choices are always challenged.

Parents of successful readers read favourite bits from the classics to their children. When a classic is serialised on television they will probably watch it with their children and get out the book.

Putting books everywhere

Parents of successful readers make sure their children have a book to read whenever they are out and they have nothing else to do. They include books in the packing for holidays and read up on the place that the family visits before or after or both. There will be a collection of books in the house that can be used for quick reference. Books on the body, insects, birds, plants, machines, history, space and the world are just some of the ones that every family should aim to have on their bookshelf. Cut-price bookshops are a good source of these handy reference books.

The family will have books and magazines by the bed. Parents encourage children to have a book on the go. Their children see bedtime as a chance to read for a while. Reading is used as a respite from family time. Time is given over to reading as well as watching television or using computers.

You can encourage reading but you cannot force it

Not every parent who provides an environment that should produce a successful reader will produce children who want to read. It is important to realise that you are only offering your children opportunities and they will select from those you offer and those that are available elsewhere. Even if what you offer is rejected, it is important that you have offered it: it may be taken up at a later stage.

The most important piece of advice for any parents who find themselves in this situation is, *do not panic*. Do not take your children's refusal to enjoy reading personally. You are not a failure. Go on providing all the things that have been suggested and give your children time. There are many men who took little interest in reading while they were at school but take great pleasure in reading in their adult lives. There are many women who found reading difficult and stressful at school and who are ambitious and voracious readers now they are adults. Your children will remember you as an enthusiastic reader. They will know that reading is something people can be enthusiastic about.

THE GIRL WHO LOVED LIBRARIES.

As soon as she was born, Helen's parents involved her in the pleasure that can be gained from books. As a baby she was read to; she had cloth books in the playpen; plastic books for the bath and cardboard books in her cot. She became a member of the library at the earliest possible moment. Each week she would go to the library with her parents while they chose their books. Visits to the library for Helen and her family were stress free. Everyone was eager to see what was on the shelves and to search out books that they might want to read. Helen became a keen reader.

The librarian was helpful, and Helen's enthusiasm for libraries and books went on growing. Helen looked forward to her visit all week. One of the things that fostered her enjoyment of the library was the fact that the family always went at the same time. Helen's family chose Friday. That meant she had the whole weekend to enjoy the books before the start of the routine of school and work. There was no stress about the library visits. Books were always returned on time or renewed. Helen's parents didn't have the problem of having to pay for overdue books or nag Helen to get the books back on time. Books were never lost.

Friday's visit to the library was a magical mystery tour where Helen had freedom to explore wherever she wanted. It was a chance to peek into worlds where other people lived. It was a chance to find out that people lived lives that were vastly different and remarkably similar to her own. Books gave her a sense of adventure and curiosity. They gave her an appreciation and determination to read more, to enjoy the adventure of reading.

Libraries allow children adventures of the mind where their imaginations can be given free rein and parents can be as sure, as they can anywhere, that their children are safe.

Be flexible about setting goals

Some adults have been told that children should read every word on the page, in the right order and on their own. This systematic approach to reading seems to make sense, but inflexibility can create enormous tension. The tension comes because some children cannot learn when a system is inflexible. They become:

◆ careless and just say anything that comes into their heads
◆ frightened of making mistakes

- sullen and reluctant to keep trying
- easily distracted

The result is that they feel inadequate whenever they are asked to read. They stumble more and more, eventually grinding to a halt. Parents who believe that finishing the book or the pages set is the goal can lose patience and then feel inadequate themselves. They are worried by their children's inability to read fluently and they know their efforts are not working. They just go on relentlessly. The homework has to be done.

THE BOY WHO WAS BOGGED DOWN BY DAILY READING

TRY CHANGING YOUR READING ROUTINE WHEN YOU GET STUCK IN A RUT

Jack hated reading. He couldn't read the books he brought home from school. His mum hated reading with Jack. She was distressed because she didn't know how to help him. She knew it was vital that Jack learnt to read. She also knew that it was essential that Jack should feel he could relax at home. She was in despair. She did try to do what the school wanted her to do with Jack, but the trouble was she ended up being bad-tempered and impatient. She was distressed because she wanted to be supportive. She longed to be relaxed and encouraging.

Jack's mum decided to be more flexible. She decided she wasn't going to read with Jack for a week. She sent a note to the teacher explaining that she and Jack were both so unhappy when they read together that she felt she was doing more harm than good. She had decided that a break was essential.

She told Jack that she had written the letter. She explained to him that they were having a week off from reading together. He could look at any books, including his reading book if he wanted, while she was getting tea ready. She would be happy to look at anything he showed her and to talk with him about it.

Her plan worked. She was amazed at how relaxed Jack was when he talked to her about his books. He would show her things he had noticed in the pictures and even try to read bits of the book. While Jack explored his books he and his mum enjoyed their time together. Instead of worrying about working with his mum Jack looked forward to spending some time with his books and some time with his mum.

It was crucial that when Jack relaxed his mum didn't seize the opportunity to put the reading book back in front of him. She stuck to the week off. When they began the set reading book again she allowed Jack to keep exploring. He would look at the page for quite a long time and then when he had something to tell her they would discuss it. Sometimes it would be something about the picture, sometimes it would be something about a word and sometimes his mum would ask him questions. What is the longest word on the page? What is the shortest sentence? Jack was now realising that reading was about looking and thinking. He knew he could do that. He started to love reading. As he looked he got lots of ideas about what the words might say and became interested to see if the words on the page had anything to do with his ideas. When he was allowed to go at his own pace and given the chance to explore and use his imagination, his reading blossomed. He became fascinated about having the key to finding out so much. Reading became satisfying. He had the chance to think his own thoughts, read the thoughts of someone else and have fun.

5 steps to take the stress out of reading with your children

If your children are getting miserable and you are getting frustrated when you read together, follow these steps.

1   Take yourself out of the situation. Jack's mum stopped the reading book.
2   Let your children choose some reading material. It could be a book, a comic or the TV guide.
3   Get them to tell you something about it.
4   Develop your ability to be interested in what your children are saying. Curb your need to take over.
5   Listen to how your children describe the story or the pictures. You may learn something about the book or about how they understand what they see.

What to do when you get stuck

Many parents feel totally confused when their children struggle with reading. They don't give up. They try to help their children make progress in reading even when their hard work seems to go nowhere. They go into school to try to sort the problem out even if they are embarrassed. They never give up even when persisting makes them feel completely hopeless.

If you feel hopeless sometimes there are things you can try. You might be surprised at how successful you are. You might find out just what the problem is when others who seemed to know more, couldn't.

All readers need to know:

♦   the letter sounds and the letter names. The sound the 'a' makes in 'mat' is different to the sound it makes in 'mate'

- that some of the letters are vowels and the rest are consonants
- that 'y' is a vowel when it says 'e' on the end of a word like 'baby' or 'I' on the end of a word like 'sky' or 'i' in a word like 'mystery'
- how to say all the letters clearly
- that the letter on the left-hand side of the word is invariably the first sound of the word
- that the letter at the right-hand side of the word is often the last sound
- that where an 'e' is the last letter but not the last sound as in 'cake', the last consonant will be the last sound
- that words can be split into syllables
- that each syllable has one spoken vowel sound
- that words are grouped together in ways that make sense
- that books are written using sentences that make sense
- that sentences are written using words that make sense
- that the words on the page will have something to do with the picture or the title of the story, or what has gone before
- that the title of the story matters

There will be other things that readers need to know. This list gives you some things to think about. Not every problem is complicated. Sometimes it is quite simple.

THE BOY WHO DIDN'T KNOW THE SOUNDS

Sam was a small child for his age with babyish features. Even when Sam was eight people responded to him as if he was a cute four-and-a-half-year-old. When Sam failed to learn to read it was assumed that he:

- *was immature*
- *had a learning difficulty*
- *was lazy*
- *had low intelligence*

Or it could have been that he was often away from school? To improve his reading he was given easy books to read that he could manage, worksheets for matching that he could manage, two-letter words to learn that he mostly managed, practice with jigsaws and handwriting practice. Despite many hours of individual or small group attention Sam still failed to read. He couldn't spell his own surname.

From the age of six there had been a noticeable improvement in his general schoolwork, although he was still performing well under the academic level for his age. One day, just by chance, Sam's mother realised that Sam did not know all the letter names or the letter sounds that went with each letter he wrote. She tried getting him to spell a few words. The only words he did know he had learnt by remembering how they looked and so he could get them right even though he didn't know the sounds. No one had realised that any words he could read he had memorised. His improvement was lopsided. It was also slow.

Sam's mother explained what she had noticed to his teacher. His teacher was then able to make some suggestions to Sam's mother.

◆ *Each time Sam makes a mistake on a word, get him to make the sound of each letter in the word. He needs to make the sounds clearly so there is a definite difference between one sound and another.*
◆ *Next get Sam to spell out the same word using the alphabet names.*
◆ *Once he can tell you the sounds of the letters and the names of the letters see if he can work out what the word is.*
◆ *Don't worry if he stumbles. Allow him time to learn. Everyone can find learning something new difficult.*

Sam began to make steady progress. Before Sam's mother had recognised where his difficulty lay, Sam had been tested for his reading. His score was so low that he was classed as a non-reader. When he was tested three months later Sam had improved enough to be classed as a reader with a reading age of a seven-year-old.

What other people did that helped Sam become a reader

When Sam had a problem reading people thought Sam was the problem. Now whenever there is a problem people realise that there is something Sam does not know, and they check to find out what it could be. Then they teach Sam the information that he is missing. Sam finds it easy to learn when people are teaching him as if he can learn.

How Sam changed

In the past Sam was in the habit of making wild guesses. Now he makes educated guesses. He looks at the letters of the word in front of him and gets as many clues as he can. He thinks about what he has already read and decides what word could possibly fit in this place and in this story. He is using context as well as what he knows about the sounds letters can make.

Understanding the different sounds of letters

Letters are dynamic. They change their sound depending on where they are. For example the sound 'p' makes in 'pup' is quite different than the sound it makes in 'phone'. The sound 'c' makes in 'cat' is not the same as the sound it makes in 'ice' and the sound 't' makes in 'top' bears no resemblance to the sound it makes in 'the'. Some children need this information to be explained to them many times. They are not slow learners but at an early age they may have decided that each letter only had one sound. They haven't noticed all the evidence to the contrary. It has been ignored or just seen as confusing.

You can help children who are not developing as readers, because they think all letters have the same sound all the time. Get them to:

- ◆ choose a letter
- ◆ search for words in their reading book that have that letter
- ◆ write down the words
- ◆ say the words out loud

◆ tell you the sound the letter is making in each word. Sometimes the letter may combine with another letter to make a sound

Most children don't learn how to do this in one session. Give your children the chance to practise whenever they need to and eventually they will recognise how to read the letter wherever they find it.

Sounds of groups of letters

◆ If children have learnt the simple sounds for 'h', 't', 'e' and 'a', then they can put 'h', 'a' and 't' together to make 'hat'.
◆ Without extra knowledge they will not be able to put 't', 'h' and 'e' together to make 'the'. Since none of the simple sounds can be combined to make 'th' children need to learn that putting a 't' and an 'h' together makes a new sound, 'th'. There are more sounds than there are individual letters.
◆ Sometimes parents think that because children can read 'the' they should be able to read 'this', 'that' and 'then'. It seems simple but it isn't. Some children will learn 'the' as a whole word. When they see those letters coming together they will know the word is 'the' but they will not be able to put 'the' with another letter like 'n' and read 'then'. Although they know the word 'the' they do not know what sound 'th' makes. When children do know what sound 'th' makes then they can gradually work out other words that have that letter combination.
◆ Examples of other groups of letters children can learn the sound of are 'ch', 'sh' and 'tion', as in chips, shop and station.

Push on with polysyllabic words

If children are to succeed in exams and tests to the maximum of their capability they will have to learn the strategies that everyone uses when they read a long word. A polysyllabic word is a word with more than one syllable. A syllable is a sound bite that is part of the word. In order to read a polysyllabic word the reader will have to break the word up.

How to break up a long word

◆ See whether the word contains any little words you already know. In a word like 'unforgettable' you can find 'for', 'get', 'table', 'able' and 'forget'.

◆ Check the vowels 'a', 'e', 'i', 'o', 'u', and don't forget 'y'. Every syllable has one vowel that is spoken. Not every vowel is spoken. In the word 'recommend' each vowel is spoken and there are three syllables. In the word 'dreaming' the 'a' is not spoken. There are three vowels but only two syllables.

◆ Decide what effect each vowel is having on the letters around it. In the word 'sauce' the 'a' combines with the 'u' to make the 'or' sound. The 'e' combines with the 'c' to make the 's' sound.

◆ See if there are any strings of letters like 'ing', 'nce' or 'tion'.

◆ Notice whether the word has a prefix. A prefix is some letters added on to the front of a word. You can put 'in' at the front of 'side' to make 'inside'.

◆ Notice whether the word has a suffix. A suffix is added to the end of a word. You can put 'ing' on the end of 'jump' to make 'jumping'.

◆ Look at the first and last letter, think about the context and try to predict what the word might be.

Encourage your children to explore different methods to break up the word and work out how to read it. They may not use the same one each time and it may not be the same strategy as you would use.

How breaking up words helps thinking

Children who are taught to break up words develop their thinking. They learn techniques that will help them become independent and responsible for their own learning. When words are broken up they learn how to deconstruct an idea and reconstruct it. Children who are successful in exams and tests will know how to use everything they have learnt, in as many ways as possible, to the greatest advantage.

Work on words to widen your world

If children use a wide vocabulary they stand a better chance of doing well in exams and tests. Their vocabulary should include everyday words and specialist vocabulary that people use on particular occasions or at particular times. The more children hear new words spoken in a meaningful way the more chance they have of being able to read and understand those words.

◆ Encourage your children to use the specialist vocabulary that goes with their interests.
◆ Enrich their vocabulary – make a conscious effort to use new words.
◆ Hunt out classics of children's literature.
◆ Use the library.
◆ Have a dictionary and thesaurus suited to your children's ability as well as ones for you to use at home.

Children who do well in exams and tests know that their language is rich and varied. They expect to come across words that they have never heard of and they expect to find out what those words mean. Children who are introduced to lots of words will be comfortable exploring the possibilities and enchanted by the chance to learn more and explore further.

We live in a multi-cultural world. Make sure your children get experience of other cultures through books.

Even tiny children can share vocabulary when you look at picture books together.

Sentences make sense

Children who use full sentences are easy to understand. They make it possible for others to follow what they are trying to say. They want what they say to make sense. They put in detail so they can be understood. Because they have experience of sentences making sense they expect what they read to make sense.

How to encourage children to read sense

Some children don't expect what they read to make sense. They will quite happily read out loud complete 'gobbledygook'. You can correct this problem.

1 Ask questions before your children start to read.
2 Prompt children to think about what they are about to read. The questions you ask will arise from what you can see in the book. You could ask questions about:

   ◆ the characters
   ◆ what is about to happen
   ◆ the front cover
   ◆ what the children have read already

By asking questions you are developing your children's ability to think about what they are reading. As they develop their thinking they will expect what they hear or read or say to make sense. As they develop their thinking their reading will improve. As their reading improves their learning in all subjects will improve. As their learning improves so will their success in exams and tests.

Beware. Some children with hearing problems do not hear words that are not emphasised. When they speak they often don't say those words. When they read they assume those words don't need to be read so they leave them out. The problem disappears when children realise all the words written down in their reading book are part of the story.

Children who make it up as they go along

Some children haven't realised that when an adult is reading to them the adult is looking at the printed word and it is the print that tells the story. These children think that the adult is making up the story and so when they come to read they make up a story as well. This can be corrected by asking children to point out words that are written on the paper. If the children point to each word as they read they soon become aware that there is a story written down. Reading is saying the words that are written down. If they learn how to do it well the story will make sense.

Punctuate to illuminate

Some children can get all the words right when they are reading and understand what they have read. Some children can get all the words right when they are reading but not understand what they have read.

Pausing properly for punctuation is essential for understanding. If children don't stop at a full stop their sentences run together, and the meaning is lost.

Children need to learn that a full stop means the idea is completed.

In the early books from the reading schemes full stops often coincide with the end of the line. Children automatically pause there. As the reading level increases and the sentences become longer the sentences may begin and end anywhere on the line. If children haven't realised that the full stop is telling them to pause, their reading suffers. They may continue to pause at the end of a line, or at the end of a paragraph, and nowhere else.

It is simple to correct this by pointing out to children how full stops work. You can reinforce punctuation when children copy out a paragraph from the reading book. Get them to start each new sentence on a new line. They will have to hunt for the full stops to know when to start the new line.

Have a breather

Some children read as much as they can on one breath. It is tiring for them and for the person listening to them. You can help them overcome this problem by reminding them to take a breath at the beginning of every sentence and, if they need one, at a comma.

Speak with care and clarity

It is important to recognise that you may be the only person who speaks clearly and precisely to your children. You need to check that your children speak clearly and precisely to you. Your children will have a better chance when they come to learn to read if they know how to pronounce words clearly. Children who say 'dis', 'dat' and 'de' instead of 'this', 'that' and 'the' are going to find it difficult to work out what words with 'th' in them might mean. Clear pronunciation doesn't help to work out every single word when you read but it does help with many of them.

Concentrating on what you are reading

Children who can concentrate on their reading can finish their work quickly and with fewer mistakes. They know:

◆ that they are supposed to be responsible
◆ how to get back on track when their minds have drifted off
◆ how to keep going even if they want to do something else

Children who can't focus on their reading sometimes think that the reading is just something that happens alongside other things that take their attention. They think it is fine to stop reading and tell you about something that has happened or something they want. They ask what the time is because they don't want to miss out on the next thing they have planned.

The best way to cope with children who are distracted easily is to set the limits of the task. They need to know how much has to be done before they can go and do anything else. It is important to set a quantity because children who are distracted easily can use up so much of your energy that you just want to stop the activity so you can get some peace. If you persevere, and you will if you keep remembering how important it is for everyone to understand their responsibilities and fulfil them, you will find your children begin to take on the attitudes you are teaching. It takes some children a long time to absorb this need to be responsible, but it is an essential skill and therefore it is critical that adults teach it.

How to help a careless reader

Careless readers haven't realised that reading precisely is important if they are going to enjoy what they read. Reading accurately is important in exams and tests.

You can encourage your children to read accurately by keeping a tally of mistakes they make in one paragraph. Challenge them to see if they can reduce the number of mistakes. Before they begin, ask them to think about how they are going to make sure they will do better this time.

Children who do well in exams and tests are children who learn how to assess ways they can improve and find ways of practising so that the improvement will happen.

Helping the slow reader

Children who read slowly need help to understand that some words, phrases and names in their books will reappear regularly. They need to be helped to realise that everything in a book is not unpredictable. As they get better at predicting, their speed will increase and so will their understanding of what they are reading. Taking it in turns to read a sentence with your children, where you read to a full stop and then they read the next sentence, will increase their pace, their expression, their understanding and their anticipation. They will pick up from you that there is a way of reading that makes reading entertaining and desirable.

Staying in control when children read deliberately badly

Some children have found ways to make sure that adults will read the minimum with them. They have found a way of reading which is so aggravating that adults have to stop the reading session in order to preserve their own sanity or avoid losing their temper and jumping up and down on the reading book . . . or the children.

One tactic that children use that drives parents mad is to sound out every single word letter by letter and then read the word looking up at the adult each time to check that the word is correct. This is bad enough in an easy reading book with only five words on a page but when children do it with later reading books, it is too much to bear.

You have to retrieve your adult position. You can be pretty sure that children who can sound out the word and then get it right many times can probably read it without sounding it out. Explain to your children that sentences should be read fluently and you are going to give them the chance to practise fluency.

3 sentences to fluency

1 Children read and repeat the first sentence until they are fluent and there are no mistakes.
2 Now they read the second sentence. If they are fluent on the second sentence they will not need to read it again.
3 If they revert to letter by letter for the second sentence make sure they read that sentence until they are fluent and then go back and start at the beginning again. Do not progress to sentence three until they are fluent in sentences one and two.

If you keep the reading session in your control, as you will if you use this method, you will feel less stressed. When you feel less stressed your children will realise that the techniques they had for getting out of reading aren't needed any more.

Fluency – a stepping stone to success

Once children realise that there is satisfaction in doing something well they become motivated.

- When they become motivated they are interested in learning.
- When they are interested in learning they learn more.
- When they learn more they increase their chances of being successful in exams and tests.

Encouraging your children to make connections

Children who make connections in their own lives look for connections in what they are reading. They have the strategies to understand more. They are motivated to use their experience and test whether one event is connected to another.

When a child goes out for the day, that is connected to getting dressed and coming home. A car accident in the street could be connected to the dog that ran out and the ambulance that took the passenger, who was in the car, to hospital. The family meal is connected to the shopping and the washing-up.

Children who don't make connections need prompting every step of the way. They are not stupid, but they can't reach their potential because they are satisfied with understanding very little. They don't make connections in their own lives and so can't make connections when they are reading. They will read a sentence and be quite happy for it to have no connection with anything they have read before in the book. They don't seem to notice when what they are reading makes no sense.

If you help your children make connections in everyday life they will look for connections when they are reading. If you ask them questions about what they are reading they will gradually realise that they can find answers to questions when they read. Connections with their world help them make connections in their brain. Connections in their brain mean they have more brain power.

How to make your children strong readers

Strong readers will be reading all the time and making connections between what they know and what they have read. Strong readers will be in a strong position when it comes to exams and tests. They will read the question carefully and know how to get the most out of the question to help in the answers. Strong readers can:

- read polysyllabic words
- use punctuation when they are reading
- draw on a wide vocabulary
- have a go at words they have not met before
- make sense of what they read
- control their breathing so that their reading is fluent
- vary their speed of reading
- use what they know to make sense of what they are reading
- stay focused on what they are reading because they are so absorbed in it
- be fascinated by what they read, wherever it is
- see reading as a challenge

A strong reader knows that understanding doesn't necessarily come word by word or even sentence by sentence. It might take several readings before the full meaning of what is being read is understood.

Strong readers who stop improving

Strong readers can plateau. They can stop developing. They start to choose easy books because they know they can read those quickly. They may continue to read a lot but they don't improve their reading. They may stop wanting to read anything they can't read easily.

A plateau can happen at any time and for many reasons. The danger for children comes when they think that the plateau they are on, is the peak. They think there is nowhere else to go. Then, if they come across reading that is challenging, they are tempted to dismiss it as boring.

20 reasons for children reaching a plateau in reading

1 They can't read tricky words – 'through', 'enough', 'psychology'.
2 They can't see little words in big words – 'fortnight', 'comfortable', 'beside', 'indifferent'.
3 They can't read polysyllabic words.
4 Their vocabulary is too limited to recognise what a word could be from the context.
5 They don't realise all the sounds a particular letter might make.
6 They don't recognise the sounds a particular group of letters might make.
7 They don't realise that what they are reading is their language written down.
8 They don't realise the importance and significance of punctuation.
9 They read too slowly to make any sense of what they are reading.
10 They don't anticipate what might come next so they see every word separately and decode it letter by letter.
11 They don't recognise that what they have already read might help them read the next bit.
12 They don't breathe correctly so they are unable to read with expression.
13 They read carelessly and don't bother to go back to make sense of what they are reading.
14 They don't realise how much attention they need to pay to read accurately and they let their minds wander.
15 They think good readers should read fast. They only read things they can read fast and stop making progress.
16 They speak sloppily so they don't recognise that the words on the page are the same as the words they speak.

:

17 They are only prepared to try books they think they can read.
18 They don't realise they can get better.
19 They don't realise that if they are to improve they have to do something about it.
20 They have not been taught the skills they need to get better. They are being listened to and they can do their reading homework, but there is no challenge.

Hard-working children can plateau too

It sometimes happens that hard-working children don't make the progress they should. Nobody realises they are having a problem. Everyone will assume they are working to the limit of their potential. If they are not making progress there will be a reason. If hard-working children are always given work that is well within their capabilities the reason why they are not improving may never be spotted. Everyone may be satisfied with their exam and test results but the children will be capable of much more. They are stuck on a plateau.

How to help your children move off a plateau

1 Listen to your children read:

- ◆ instructions from maths books
- ◆ what they have written in their homework diary
- ◆ definitions from dictionaries
- ◆ information from encyclopedias

2 Share, by reading with your children:

- books you have chosen
- books they have chosen
- books that are easy
- books that are difficult

3 Explain to your children that if they want to do well in exams and tests they have to be prepared to explore. They need to widen their horizons and increase their depth of knowledge. Explain to them that the more they read and the more different things they read, the stronger they will become as readers. They need to know it is like being an athlete. Athletes train so that they can operate at their peak in particular situations. They are capable of operating brilliantly or at least doing very well in most situations that require athleticism. Your children need to train and develop their reading so they can read brilliantly and reach undreamed-of peaks in what they read.

CHAPTER 14

MATHS TRICKS

Success in maths brings success in many exams

When children are at secondary school nearly all the subjects they do will involve maths in some way. In geography they will use co-ordinates to read maps and compasses to find direction. They will do surveys and charts. In chemistry they will need to work out quantities when they are doing experiments. In technology they will need to measure and calculate amounts. In information technology they will be making spread sheets. In history they will be producing time-lines. In physics they will have to work out how fast things go and the direction they are going in.

Fear of maths

Many children are fearful of maths – and so are many parents! People who have developed a fear of maths don't feel they can understand maths at all. They dread ever being put in a position where they will have to use their mathematical knowledge. These people are probably using maths every day. They could be calculating how much wood they need, how much paint to buy, following a knitting pattern or budgeting for the family holiday. They don't recognise that the methods they are using to cope with maths in their everyday life could also be used to cope with the maths they think is difficult.

If you feel that your maths is not good enough for you to help your children, think of the times you use maths successfully in any day. If you can teach your own children to make use of the maths you use you will have given them a good grounding for when they are learning maths away from you.

10 things any parent can teach

1 How to count forwards and backwards.
2 That some things are heavier than other things.
3 That some things are lighter than others.
4 How to tell the time.
5 How to read a timetable.
6 That distance is measured in metres.
7 That weight is measured in kilogrammes.
8 That liquids are measured in litres.
9 That things cost money.
10 What pocket money will buy.

Maths homework

Children who can cope with maths homework will have parents who know how to encourage their children to:

◆ look at the symbols in the sum. It is easy to make a mistake in maths if you don't notice what the symbol is telling you to do. The earliest mathematical symbols are $+, -, \div, \times, =$. When children feel they know how to use these they will feel relaxed when they meet other symbols in secondary school
◆ look at the numbers in the sum
◆ think about what the answer will be, compared to the numbers in the question. In early maths the answer will be bigger than the numbers in the question if the symbol says to multiply or add. The exception is when one of the numbers to be multiplied is 0. When the symbols mean that the numbers have to be divided or subtracted the answer will be smaller than one of the numbers in the question. When children learn to predict whether the answer will be greater or smaller than the numbers they started with, they will have one way of checking whether or not their answer is sensible

- check whether the answer is right. In an **add sum**, take one of the numbers added away from the answer. That should leave you with the other number that was added. In a **take away sum**, add the answer to the number you took away and that should give you the larger number. In a **division sum**, multiply the answer by the number you divided by and you'll get the starting number. In a **multiplication sum**, divide your answer by either of the numbers you multiplied and you should get the other number
- check where a mistake might have happened

Encouraging children to work neatly

Children who set their work out neatly and show how they have reached an answer will learn maths more easily than those who write numbers untidily and scatter their working out around the page.

Parents who encourage their children to do a rough draft of their maths homework develop their children's confidence because their children will know they can experiment with different ways of answering the sum, without making a mess of their books. It is important to have a neat maths book but if children think that their first effort has to be neat and right, they could be sowing the seeds of their own failure.

THE GIRL WHO MISSED THE POINT

How a bright child can start to fail

Jenny had always got her sums right. She was quicker than everybody else and she was neater than everybody else as well, until it came to long division. She liked her page to be neat and she was used to sums taking up no more than three or four lines.

When she had a sum like 5,652 divided by 36, she wanted to be able to do it so that there would be no working out, except what she could do in her head. She started off by working out that there were no 36s in 5 so she would have to work out how many 36s in 56. This was okay. There was 1. She put down 1 as the first part of her answer. The next bit she had to do was, how many 36s in 205. She started to work it out in her head. She kept getting lost. While she was doing it in her head other children were writing down their working out and moving on. They had discovered there were 5 lots of 36 in 205 and 25 left over.

Jenny was completely stuck. As the other children overtook her she got more muddled and became flustered. Jenny's confidence had gone, and so for the time being had her chances of being successful in maths.

Children whose confidence goes are in danger of deciding that:

◆ they are not as 'good' as they thought they were
◆ they hate maths
◆ they are no good at maths
◆ if the teaching had been any good they would know how to do it without spoiling their page with working out
◆ anything that makes them feel this bad should be avoided
◆ maths doesn't matter

THE BOY WHO GOT THE POINT

How a slow child can start to succeed

Paul had never been very good at maths. Other people were quicker and neater. Other people seemed to get the right answer without having to check. He wasn't very good at multiplication and so he was hopeless at division. He could do his two times table and his one times table and he could add and take away, but after that he was always shaky. His mum showed him a way he could work out all his tables by using his one times and his two times tables.

When he did 5,652 divided by 36 he started by writing

out the first two sums of his 36 times table. 1 x 36 = 36,
2 x 36 = 72. He then realised that he could get 1 lot of 36
out of 56 and there would be 20 left over.

The next bit of the sum he had to do was how many 36s
in 205. He hadn't gone far enough in his 36 times table
so he added the answers for the 1 x 36 and the 2 x 36
together to find out 3 x 36. He realised this wasn't enough
so he doubled the 2 x 36 to find out what 4 x 36 was. He
found that this still wasn't high enough so he added the
2 x 36 and the 3 x 36 together to find out what 5 x 36
was. He thought this was probably right but he doubled 3
x 36 just to check. That was more than he needed so he
was right. He did only need 5 x 36. He worked out that
there were 25 left over.

He now had to find out how many 36s there were in
252. He added the answer to 6 x 36 to 1 x 36 and found
that the answer to that was just what he needed. He had
the right answer, 157.

Paul was delighted with his success. He had written
down what he had used to help him get the right answer
and he had written it neatly. He felt confident that he
could use the same method to find the answer to any long
division sum. Paul's self-esteem had arrived and so had
his chances to develop his mathematical ability and reach
his full potential.

Children who find a way to work out sums using what they
know:

◆ start to enjoy maths
◆ feel confident when they are given something new to learn
◆ use the knowledge they have to learn something new
◆ are prepared to experiment with different techniques to find
  the answer
◆ know that they won't always predict the right answer the first
  time but every prediction gives them a bit more information

Give your children the tools and teach them how to use them

1 Do workings out on paper. Don't try to do it all in your head.
2 Use a sharp pencil and have a supply of sharp pencils to hand.
3 When you are working on scrap paper cross out what is wrong and do it again, no matter how small the mistake.
4 When you transfer work to your exercise book, copy it carefully and check.
5 Make sure when you set out your work that you can read it easily and so can everyone else. Children often go through a phase of minuscule handwriting. This is a good time to point out to them how important it is that anything they write is clear enough for them to be able to check. How they present their work matters, not just to their teacher. It could be crucial if they misread a number they have written and end up getting the wrong answer. By asking children to read to you what they have written they will realise the difficulties that poorly presented work can cause.

Reasons why children panic about maths

◆ They don't understand maths.
◆ They don't know the basics.

Preparation for mental maths tests

If you want to help your children, the first thing you need to find out is what is meant by mental maths in your children's school.

In some schools mental maths is, as many adults remember, sums presented in a simple way and the answer written down. For example 7x3=? How many centimetres in a metre? John is 13, Mary is 9, how much older is John?

In a drive to increase the level of mathematical skills experts are insisting that children learn to deal with more complex maths, mentally. Now questions are likely to be, 'Two children go to a theme park. It costs them £7.50 each to get in and they each have an ice cream for £1.25. How much change will they have from £20?'

How to help your children prepare for mental maths

Teach them how to listen carefully. Find a set of questions. Your children might bring home sheets of questions from school or you could buy or make up a set.

1 Read out the first question.
2 Your children write down what you have said. At this stage the children do not answer the question. You are giving them practice at listening to the question and hearing the information in the question. Many children don't realise how to listen or what to listen to in a maths question. When they write down what you have said they are learning how to focus on what is important in the question.
3 Read all the questions before any are answered.
4 Each time you read, your children should write down the question.
5 Your children will get faster at writing down the questions. They will be becoming familiar with mental maths questions. Repetition promotes confidence. Confidence from repetition promotes panic-free learning.
6 Use the same questions again and this time get your children to write down the sum that they will use to work out the answer to the question. Your children do not answer the questions yet. Moving from the words that describe the question to the numbers that describe the question encourages children to see there is a process that makes sense. They will gradually learn how to use this process themselves. Children who panic will be able to work out how to get a sensible answer. Your children

will understand what is meant when people say, 'Just think about the question.'

7 The next stage is to do the sums that have just been written.

8 Now, you read out the questions again and the children, on a fresh piece of paper, see if they can answer the questions correctly, as if they were doing a mental maths test in school.

This method works because you have made mental maths questions familiar to your children. Children will be relaxed enough to work out what they have been asked to do.

Some children seem to be naturally good at maths. When they see anything mathematical they are confident that it makes sense, even if they are not sure how to do it straight away. Other children find maths completely incomprehensible. From the very earliest stages it is a complete mystery.

Maths is a craft that children can enjoy

Teach your children how to rule a straight line and you will have lifted their skill base dramatically. If they can rule a straight line between two points they will know how to:

◆ hold the ruler steady
◆ hold the ruler so their finger doesn't get in the way
◆ focus on the point of the pencil
◆ recognise the importance of the starting and finishing point
◆ impose control on a number of things at once – the pencil, the paper, the ruler, their hands

Teach your children how to fold a square of paper in half so they can make a triangle or a rectangle. If they can fold a square in half they will understand how to:

- recognise a corner
- line up two matching edges
- take care
- cope with a two-dimensional task
- watch their hands and control what they are doing

Teach your children how to cut with scissors along a straight line that has been drawn or folded. If they can use scissors to cut a straight line they will understand how to:

- control both hands when each hand is doing something slightly different
- keep watching where the scissors are moving so that they can make minor adjustments to keep the cutting accurate
- keep control of what they are cutting
- cope with a task that is happening away from a table
- improve their hand, arm and eye control

Teach your children how to use a pair of compasses to draw a circle. When they can draw a circle they understand how to control their:

- wrist, hand and fingers while using a tool
- hand so that they apply the right amount of pressure
- pace to get the result they want

Children who are taught how to use a pencil, ruler and scissors use them many times because they get pleasure from being able to use them and use them well. This means that they practise and develop activities for themselves that come from being able to do these basic skills. Many craft activities demand precision at the early stages. Craft activities are based on mathematics. Children who do craft activities use mathematics in real life.

Maths is a language

Some students who are successful at maths are able to work out the answers just by looking at the numbers. To them the numbers and the symbols make sense. They think in numbers. Numbers are as meaningful to them as anything else in their world.

Many other students, who are successful at maths, make words their focus. They have to put each mathematical thought into a sentence. They need to link the numbers to words. If you have children who can do mathematics through numbers alone they may not need much help from you. For children who need words to understand maths it is important to teach them mathematical language.

Mathematical language is mainly everyday language. 'The Maths teacher gave us some homework today that is not due in until next Tuesday. That means I have six days to get it done, but because I am going away for the weekend I really haven't got that much time to get it finished.' In this sentence there are different mathematical ideas: Today is a beginning and next Tuesday is an ending. There is a total number of days and some subtractions that have to be done from the total.

Word games are a good way of teaching the language of maths. For example, you can show that maths attracts opposites through words.

1 Think of all the pairs of words that are opposites. Pairs like fast and slow, rich and poor, fat and thin, black and white, up and down.
2 Find all the pairs that are to do with maths. Long and short, light and heavy, up and down, horizontal and vertical, add and subtract.

Maths is an art

Some children who are good at art love maths. They see the shape and form of graphs, squares and cubes, triangles and pyramids. They explore maths by exploring what shapes are, what they can be used for and how they look. They put numbers to the things they see and rearrange the things they see to make different patterns. They look for patterns and they are intrigued by them.

If your children like art but do not like maths, get them a geometry set, some coloured pencils and some graph paper. They can explore what they can do with them. Dot to dots, colouring books and puzzle books are all good sources of maths activities. Origami and mosaic books encourage mathematical thinking.

Maths is history

Some children will enjoy exploring maths once they know that maths has a history. They are fascinated to know what people in the past found out. They are amazed to discover what people did before there were . . . clocks and watches, calculators, rulers, money, pairs of compasses, map references and ways of measuring distance, length or weight.

Look out for books that explain how things were calculated in the past and why it was done in that way. Keep an eye out for TV programmes or newspaper articles about new discoveries.

Maths basics

Maths is a way of ordering our world. Children need to know that when they are ordering their world they are using maths. When they put their shoes in pairs, work out how many weeks it takes to save for something, find out how long a journey takes, make a model, they are using maths to plan and to organise. Children are using maths all day and every day. Once they know that that is what they are doing, maths starts to be easy.

Maths is about relationships

Children can learn that numbers are linked. Every number can be linked to another number. They just have to think about how. There are links between five and ten. One link is that five is half of ten. Another link is that five plus five makes ten. Which links can they think of? Which links can they make between the digits in their telephone number? This game of making links can be used at whatever level of maths you are studying. Children who are successful at maths learn to make links. Children who are unsuccessful only look for an answer.

Revising for maths tests and exams

The best way to revise for maths is to work through questions. The best questions to work through come with an example of how to do that type of question. Answers in the back of the book are a great help because when children see what the answer should have been, they can go back through their work and find out where they went wrong. The difference between someone who is good at maths and someone who isn't is that someone who is good at maths has a lot of practice.

If your children want to do well in mathematics they must do lots of examples of each new thing they learn. Very few children can excel at mathematics without doing any work.

CHAPTER 15

SPELLING TRICKS

Helping your children to think about spelling

Most people who think about spelling can find ways of making sure they always get their spelling right. People who think spelling is important increase their chances of becoming good spellers. Children who think their spelling is important will do well. When spelling is part of family time children will see spelling as important.

Making spelling a family matter

When you include spelling as one of the things your family does together, you can:

◆ make sure your children are thinking
◆ check whether your children are pronouncing words correctly and saying them clearly
◆ look up unusual words in the dictionary
◆ help your children realise that when they learn one word they are close to knowing lots of words

Preparing for spelling tests was always fun in the Robinson house. Everyone sat down to do it for twenty minutes and everyone did each other's list. There was Peter who was twelve, Natasha eight and Becky six. Of course Becky couldn't manage all of the words on everybody's lists but she became very confident that learning to spell was something she could do.

Everyone was supportive of each other. Everyone thought of ways to make remembering the spelling possible. Everyone joined in discussions about words and their meanings and why those particular words were on people's spelling lists.

How to help your children prepare for spelling tests

1 Ask your children to read the list to you.
2 Make sure each word is pronounced clearly.
3 Ask your children to decide which words they think they already know.
4 Test your children on the whole list.
5 If they know all the words, get them to look up the dictionary and find out what the words mean.
6 If there are any mistakes, ask them to list the words which were wrong in one column and the words they got right in another column.
7 Ask them to tell you how they are going to remember each word they got wrong.
8 Test them on the words they are not sure how to spell.
9 Add the words they have got right to the 'known' list.
10 Look again at the words that were wrong and see if there are suggestions which will mean they remember them correctly.
11 Keep going until twenty minutes has gone and see how many words they can spell correctly by the end of the time.
12 Even if your children get the words right remember to test each night so that you can spot any of the words that need extra practice.
13 Dictating sentences that use the words is a good way of making sure your children can spell the words correctly all the time.

THE BOY WHO TRIED BUT JUST WASN'T QUITE READY

Michael was five when he was given his first spelling list. The list was 'the', 'and', 'but', 'girl' and 'boy'. These words did not follow a particular spelling pattern. The teacher felt that if the children in the class knew these words they could use them in their writing and reading. Although Michael's mum tried very hard to help him learn his spellings he did not get any right when it came to the test.

HOW COULD THIS HAPPEN?

◆ Many five-year-olds are just not ready to learn how to spell words. *Do not panic.* As they get older, providing they are still being involved in how words are formed and how words are used, they will catch up.

◆ Some parents think their children have learnt the words because when they have been practising the words at home, whoever has been teaching the children has given them so many hints that the help has been more like a guessing game than spelling practice.

◆ The children may not know enough letter sounds or be able to match the sounds with the letter shapes. In practice, at home, they might remember a series of letter shapes but when they need to remember them later they can't. *Don't panic.* This is not a short-term memory problem. Your children are just not familiar enough with what they don't know. If you are patient and keep working on letter sounds and the shapes of the letters that go with them, your child will begin to make connections.

◆ The children might have all the letters right but the order wrong. They might write 'gril' instead of 'girl'. *Don't panic.* This is not an indication of dyslexia. If your children make this mistake, number the letters in each word so they associate the position of the letter with a number – 'g' is 1, 'i' is 2 and so on.

◆ The children might have all the letters in the right order but be confused about which way round some of the letters should go so write 'doy' instead of 'boy'. *Don't panic.* This is not a sign of a child with a special problem. Many children go through this phase. Show your children that many letters are based on the letter shape c; a, c, d, e, g, o, q, s. Give them practice at writing them. Make sure that as your children write each letter, they are saying the correct name or sound of the letter.

◆ When you are teaching your children the shapes and sounds of the letters, use words they know. Adam always knew which way round a 'd' or a 'b' went when he thought of his name, and so did Rebecca.

◆ The children may have written all the letters they know because they can see that other children are busy writing something. The children have not understood that spelling a word means you pick particular letters from the ones you know and put them in a particular order. *Don't panic.* This is normal. Many children take time to build up the complete understanding of anything new they are being taught.

◆ The children may not have written anything at all because they did not get started when the teacher started and then became confused. *Don't panic.* This does not mean your children are complete no-hopers. The problem might be sorted out by practising the skill of doing something at someone else's pace, at home. It is also worth checking your child's hearing. At home your child might be able to get the words right but at school where there are more sounds or they are not looking at the teacher they may miss what is being said.

THE GIRL WHO STOPPED HAVING A GO

Kelly had always got good marks for her spelling tests and the spelling in her schoolbooks was fine too. It was only when Kelly went into a new class that she began to have problems. The marks for her spelling tests plummeted. Kelly was very bad tempered at home and would not allow anyone to help her.

Why children stop having a go

◆ It could be that they can't cope with the next level of difficulty because they haven't learnt the basics. This problem often doesn't surface until the children need to use what they already know to learn something else. Children may get words like 'mother', 'her' and 'under' right every time but have never realised that the last two letters, 'er', make a particular sound. This means that when they come to spell a word like 'permanent' which only combines simple sounds like 'man' and 'ent' the children do not have any idea of how to put sounds together. *Don't panic.* There are ways to help children who have been successful and then are unsuccessful. The most important thing is that the children have a go and write something down. Then you and your children can look at what has been written, compare it to the correct version and see if you can work out what needs to be learnt next.

◆ Sometimes children don't know very much at all because they have always copied or they have had a best friend sitting next to them who has been helping them without anybody realising. *Don't panic.* Just go back to the very simplest words and find out what you need to teach. Don't expect to teach it all in a week. If you take it slowly and only teach one or two words at a time you will keep noticing where the gaps are and you will be able to think of ways of filling them in.

◆ Sometimes children are affected by their new teacher. Perhaps the teacher shouts, has a different accent or speaks too quickly. *Don't panic.* Before you rush to the school to complain, just think about how you could help your children cope. It is important children learn strategies for coping. You cannot make the world perfect for your children so it is important they learn how to adapt. Your children can learn not to be frightened by a teacher who shouts.

Why do some children confuse the sound of letters?

> *Nazim was learning his spellings. He spelt 'must' as
> 'musd' and 'star' as 'sdar'. Although he could remember
> for a minute how to spell the words, when he was on his
> own he would go back to putting a 'd' instead of a 't'.
> Nazim's mum had battles with this problem every week
> when she tried to help him with his spelling.*

It is often difficult to understand why your children are getting
something wrong, but once you discover where the confusion
is you can see why the confusion is happening. Nazim's confusion was understandable when you realise that 'test' sounds
the same as 'pressed'. For Nazim the misunderstanding was
the difference between 't' and 'd'. Once he knew that 'd' never
followed 's' he could spell words with 'st'.

Remember Nazim when your children come home with
something they can't do. Your children are not stupid and lazy
and are not deliberately trying to wind you up. They really
want to be able to understand and get on with their work but
they can't. What stops children learning something that
everyone thinks they should be able to do is usually a tiny
misunderstanding that causes a big wall of confusion.

Helping your children to think about spelling

1 Find a word that you know will be difficult for your
   children to spell.
2 Write it down.
3 Ask your children to read out the letters.
4 Ask them to tell you anything they notice.

Children might notice:

- little words in the big word
- how many letters there are in the word
- any letters that come more than once
- double letters
- silent letters
- the shape of the word

Even if what your children say sounds odd to you, write it down. People see things differently. If we want children to think about spelling we must allow them their thoughts. If we say there is only one right way of seeing things, we stop people from learning in the way they learn best and we may even stop them learning at all.

CHAPTER 16

HOW TO HELP YOUR CHILDREN PUT PEN TO PAPER

Schoolwork involves discussion, practical tasks and putting pen to paper. Success in exams depends on being able to answer written exercises. It is crucial that your children learn to manage all types of written work.

Success in written work

Children who are successful at putting pen to paper have strategies to work out what needs to be done and how to do it. Children who are confident about doing written exercises:

♦ know that there will be information to help them included in the exercise
♦ look at the title to see what the exercise is about
♦ look to see if there is an example
♦ read the instructions and then think about whether they have done anything similar before
♦ look back in the book to check they are on the right track
♦ know that if they get started they will be more likely to finish
♦ find something interesting in the exercise
♦ see the work as an opportunity to learn something new
♦ know that the way they do the work will help their teachers know what they need to teach next
♦ understand that doing the work is a valuable use of their time

THE BOY WHO KNOWS HOW TO USE
WHAT HE KNOWS

*When James is given an exercise from a book he looks at it
to see what he needs to do. He knows that written
exercises, whether they are on worksheets, in a book or from
the blackboard, all have the same outcome. He has to:*

♦ *find out what he has to do by looking at the information he
is given*
♦ *think about what the answer could possibly be*
♦ *write it down*

*Whenever he sees an exercise that is new and not like ones
he has done before he runs a quick check in his mind
about whether he can work it out himself. If he can't work
it out he goes and asks. James will tell people that the work
is easy, interesting, and just like something he did before,
or complicated but still good fun. When James can't do a
written exercise he knows that he just needs some more
teaching and then he will be successful again.*

Why are some children lacking in confidence?

Children who are not confident about written exercises may:

♦ worry about their spelling
♦ worry about their handwriting
♦ think the exercise is full of traps
♦ think written exercises are unnecessary
♦ feel intimidated by committing themselves to paper
♦ want to get everything right first time
♦ have decided you can't get it wrong if you haven't done it
♦ think teachers use exercises to work out which children are
clever, rather than to find out how to teach children in their
charge
♦ not be prepared to do anything which might give someone
the opportunity to say they are stupid
♦ not be prepared to do anything which shows they can't do it
properly

◆ not know that learning happens bit by bit and exercises are a way of checking that each bit has been understood

THE BOY WHO THINKS THAT IT IS ALL NEW AND TOO HARD

When Michael is given an exercise from a book, he looks at it and decides he can't do it. He decides he doesn't know what to do. He has decided he is never any good at written exercises and so when he realises the exercise needs him to do some writing, he switches off. Michael doesn't like writing. He doesn't realise that many exercises have things in common and are easy to do if you just get on with them. He stops thinking about the work and starts thinking about something else. When he is asked why he won't do the work he says that it is too hard, too boring, too long or he doesn't understand it. When Michael can't do an exercise he won't accept any teaching. He just grows more resentful.

It is important for children to learn how to do exercises in a relaxed and positive way because exams and tests often follow the same format as written exercises. Make sure you teach your children to relax. They will learn faster.

---

6 *steps to switching on to written work*

Always look at:

1 what the title says
2 any instructions
3 an example if there is one

Always think about

4 what the instructions mean

---

5 how you are going to start
6 what type of words you might need and how you can make sure what you say can be read and understood

10 tips for success in written exercises

1 Check whether the question has to be answered using complete sentences.
2 Remember to use punctuation.
3 Make sure you know how many questions there are in the exercise. You would be surprised at the number of marks that are lost because people forgot to turn the page over, to see whether there were any questions on the other side.
4 Make sure you know how many questions you have to answer.
5 Read through all the questions to get an idea of how the exercise has been designed so that you will know how long your answers need to be to each question.
6 If you are not sure how to spell a word, see whether it is in the exercise. If you use a word from the exercise, check that you have spelt it correctly.
7 Make sure people can read your writing.
8 Imagine if you were the teacher marking a lot of exercises how much happier you would feel when you got an exercise that was nicely laid out and easy to read. Think how irritated you would feel if the work was carelessly done and poorly laid out. You need to take care with your work to show teachers that you care about them. You want them to care about your efforts and know you care about their efforts to teach you. Teachers need positive feedback just as much as pupils do.

> **9** Check that you have actually answered the question.
> **10** Read through your answers and make sure you haven't made simple spelling mistakes or left words out.

Ideas need writing down

Most of the writers in the world write about the world as they see it. It is not necessarily the world as it is or the world anyone else wants it to be. They are making sense of their own world. Successful writers write so that other people can understand what they are saying.

Writing is a very specific skill that is difficult enough for those who want to do it. It can be terribly stressful for children when they have to write about a particular subject in a particular way, by a particular time. If you teach your children how to relax, that stress will disappear and they will become successful when they are writing their ideas down. They will have the ability to write in a way that other people can understand.

What is creative writing?

One cornerstone of good creative writing is personal experience. Another is recognising the importance of linking personal experience or understanding to the subject. If your children can add their own touches of humour, drama, tragedy and remorse to their writing the reader will be interested to read their work. The writing must make sense but it doesn't have to be predictable. If readers can see how the story or the information is unfolding they will read on. A further cornerstone of good writing is understanding the way different types of writing are structured or organised.

The different types of writing children do at school

Throughout their time at school children may have to write their ideas down as:

- imaginative stories
- factual reports
- letters
- detailed descriptions
- opinion pieces
- reviews
- notes
- coursework

These pieces may be in shortened form, expanded form or in a given number of words.

The right environment to write

Children who are good at writing their ideas down are likely to come from homes where:

- they see other people writing
- there is scrap paper
- people make shopping lists, lists of things they have to do that day, lists of what to take on holiday
- people write messages to pass on to others
- they are involved in constructing letters to teachers, grandparents, the window-cleaner
- writing thank-you letters is a matter of course
- diaries are kept
- calendars are filled in
- discussions take place about how things are going to be organised
- games are played that involve writing

Helping your children to write creatively

Your children will need to be able to write sentences, understand when to paragraph, use introductions, developments and conclusions and understand the audience they are writing for. They need to know how to structure their writing in different situations. They will not learn this all at once. Creative writing is a skill that continues to develop. Many adults stay interested in learning the skill and many professions demand high levels of writing skills.

Writing games

Parents can help children develop their ability to write ideas down by playing different games. One excellent game is Consequences. Everyone has a piece of paper and a pencil. There is a caller. The game begins with the caller telling the players to write a name and a description at the top of their pieces of paper. When they have finished they fold the top section over so it can't be read and pass their paper on to the player sitting next to them. The caller then gives the next instruction. This could be to write down where the person was. All the players write, fold their paper over and pass it on. The next instruction from the caller might be to write down what the person was doing and the last instruction could be who saw them. Callers can make up any instructions. This continues until it is decided to stop the game and the results are read aloud.

For Story Beginnings each person writes a sentence on their piece of paper. The sentence is at least five words. They pass their paper on and the next person writes a sentence that could follow from the other person's opening sentence. The papers are passed on and the game continues. After every four sentences everyone reads out what has been written so far, on each paper. It is a great game for helping children develop ways of writing. They become expert at getting a story going again when they think they have written to a dead halt.

THE BOY WHO LEARNT HOW TO WRITE MORE

Gregory was a one-sentence storywriter. If he was writing about his favourite game one sentence said everything there was to say: 'I like football because it is fun'.

When Gregory played Story Beginnings he discovered that people could write more. As he tried to join in and listened and read other people's sentences he built up his own repertoire of ways of making stories longer and keeping them interesting.

CHAPTER 17

TUTORS

What is a tutor?

A tutor is somebody who can give your children:

◆ more of what they get at school
◆ something they don't get at school

Some tutors will teach your children in the same way they are taught at school and others will be able to provide something different.

Some tutors will teach in groups while others will teach individually.

Some tutors will coach for exams and some will give general help.

Some will visit your home and teach in your house and others will teach in their own centres. Many tutors prefer to teach in their own centres or homes. Although you may feel it would be more convenient if the tutor could come to you, here are some points to consider:

◆ a tutor in his own home will be able to offer a quiet space for teaching
◆ if he tries to teach in your home there could be many interruptions from the phone, other children, pets, etc.
◆ a tutor in his own home will have materials to hand that he may need to use, such as a range of books, computers, dictionaries, reference materials
◆ if you travel to the tutor you will not have to pay the expenses of the tutor travelling to you

When does a child need a tutor?

Some children need a tutor because:

- they have missed something important
- they can't follow the teacher
- they are slower than everyone else and they don't get special help at school
- an exam is coming up

Why are you thinking about a tutor?

The first point you need to be clear about is why you are looking for a tutor. Is it because:

- everyone else has got a tutor for their children or you had one when you were at school?
- you feel you can't help your children yourself and would like someone else to keep an eye on their progress?
- your children have been off school through illness or the teacher has been absent?
- your children won't listen to you or they are amongst the youngest in the class?
- the teacher thinks they need extra help?
- you would like your children to improve their marks in the exams?
- your children have asked for help?

Can tutors be helpful?

A good tutor can make an enormous difference. If your children are struggling a good tutor should be able to:

- tell you where the problem is
- start a programme that will make a difference
- keep you up to date on the progress

Not all educational difficulties will take a long time to sort out. Sometimes you may need a tutor for a couple of weeks.

Sometimes you may need a tutor for a couple of terms. Sometimes you may need a tutor for a couple of years. You should always be able to see an improvement. If you can't see an improvement it is worth changing the tutor or stopping for some time. Your children might respond better in a different situation or at a different time. This does not mean that the tutor is no good, just that the tutoring is not working for your children at that time. Tutors are used to people coming and going.

How to find a tutor

Ask around. Parents of children in your children's class may have already used a tutor whom they can recommend. Look at postcards in shop windows or adverts in newspapers. Your library will probably have lists of tutors. Check in the phone book or on the Internet.

What to check

Is the tutor someone:

- who is prepared to talk to you?
- who is prepared to listen to you?
- who can tell you what they are going to do?
- who you feel understands your children?
- you feel you can understand?

Arrangements

Some tutors ask you to pay up front and you will lose money if your children don't attend on the day and at the time agreed. Other tutors are able to offer more flexibility. You pay up front but you can vary the time. Others only ask you to pay if you attend. Check how long the sessions are and check where the sessions will be held.

Can you sit in?

Some tutors give you the chance to sit in and watch the first lesson. This will help you get a feeling for:

- the tutor's ability to teach
- the space available to teach in
- the tutor's attitude to your children
- the tutor's attitude to you
- the tutor's ability to explain things to your children and to you

Remember that when you are sitting in you are not being judged. You are there to judge whether the tutor can give you a service. Don't be embarrassed at anything the tutor finds out. You are taking your children to a third party because you want help. Wanting help shows you are taking parenting seriously. It doesn't mean you have been an irresponsible parent. It doesn't mean that you have failed your children. All parents need help at some time. Tutors are just one form of help that parents can use.

How to get value for money from a tutor

1 Take your children regularly. The tutor will think about your children before they arrive and after they go. He will be planning the best course of action. If your children attend regularly, planning and action will be uninterrupted and your children will get an excellent service. If the tutor doesn't know whether you are going to turn up or when you are going to turn up, he will have to check every time where your children are up to. You will still get good service but your children will probably not make progress quite as fast as they would if they attended regularly.
2 If the tutor is coming to your home to work with your children, ensure that the space they are working in is quiet and comfortable, with good lighting.
3 Be interested in what your children have been doing with the tutor. Listen to the tutor's explanations about the work.

4 Be realistic about how much written work you can expect. Sometimes a lot of teaching and learning is going on but there is not a lot to show for it on paper. You need to have faith that the tutor will tell you the truth. Sometimes children have to go very slowly when they first learn something, but as they get the hang of it they will be able to go faster. A way of checking whether your children are learning is to ask them to explain what they have done. As the explanations get easier to understand you will know they are learning.

5 Your children need to know that you take the tutoring seriously. If you undermine the tutor you will reduce the effect the tutor can have. Discuss problems you have with the tutor, not with your children. If you are unhappy, you are better to leave and try someone else or return to that tutor at a later date.

Tutoring your own child

If you can't find a tutor you like or for some other reason you can't manage to get your children to a tutor, you can help them at home yourself. The books *Creating Kids Who Can* and *Creating Kids Who Can Concentrate* are full of practical tips to add to those you have already found throughout this book.

A good tutor will:

- be encouraging
- have a sense of humour
- set work that can be done if there is an interruption which means they have to attend to something somewhere else in the house
- plan a time for the work when there will be the least number of interruptions possible
- be flexible in how they teach. If the children are stuck they will try a different way to help
- check the work often
- change their seating position so they can see what the children are doing

Should you tell the teachers that your children have a tutor?

It can be tricky telling a teacher that your children are having extra tuition outside school. Some teachers are delighted to find that children are having extra support. Other teachers worry that parents may be wasting their money. Some teachers feel that while the children are in their class they want to know that any progress that is being made is as a result of their teaching. Some teachers worry that there might be a conflict between the way they teach and the way the tutor teaches.

Some parents would rather tell the school so their children don't feel under any stress at keeping it quiet. Some parents tell the school because they feel the school should know. Some parents prefer not to tell anyone, not even family or friends. It really is up to you.

How long should you send your children to a tutor?

Some parents like their children to go to tutors throughout their school career. Some parents only use a tutor when their children have hit a stumbling block that they can't sort out. Your children need to know that going to a tutor is a commitment. They need to know the time and the day they will be going and what they are aiming to achieve by going. Anything under six weeks is likely to be unrealistic. You have to allow some time for the tutor to find the way your children learn best.

Children can go to tutors because they are under-achieving. The reason for the under-achievement can affect how long children need to go. If it is just one or two things they don't know and the tutor finds a way to teach them quickly then you might decide to stop the sessions and use a tutor again, if there is a need at another time.

Some children have low self-esteem and it might take a couple of years for that to be sorted out. It is a good idea to make sure that you have said goodbye to the tutor when it is time to leave. It is important to remember that your tutor will understand when you are ready to stop and tutors appreciate it when they get the chance to say goodbye.

Can tutors be harmful?

Some tutors have a style of teaching that may frighten your children. Some tutors are good with some children but may not be good with your children. The important thing about tutoring is that after a reasonable time your children should feel confident in the tutor.

Tutoring will not be harmful as long as it is making your children feel more confident about what they have to do at school.

If your children are nervous about going to the tutor, ask if you can sit in for the first few minutes. Sit to one side and when you feel your children have settled say goodbye, without causing a disturbance, and leave. Your children will feel more confident and you will feel reassured about the tutor's capability. Sometimes children can make a fuss and parents get caught up. Their children sob and cling. Don't be embarrassed about this. Think about handling it another way next time.

ACHIEVING YOUR GOALS

CHAPTER 18

COPING WITH STRESS AND PANIC

How does stress start?

Stress comes when you feel trapped. As a parent you can feel trapped because your children are having a problem at school and there is no way you can sort out the problems they have. You might be having your lunch and thinking about:

◆ the awful teacher your child has
◆ the temper tantrum your child threw because fractions are 'too hard to understand'
◆ the ghastly child in your daughter's class who pinches other children
◆ the fact that your children won't do their homework and you are bound to get a letter from the school

Stress is the natural reaction to feeling trapped. The number of things parents can worry about is enormous. Children can also feel trapped at school when they haven't got the skills to cope with every situation successfully. If stress isn't overcome it can turn into panic. *But stress can be overcome.*

Paralysing panic

Panic is the feeling you get when you feel you can't cope. You decide you don't understand the situation you are in or about to be in. You don't believe that you have any resources you can draw on at all, either within yourself or outside. Panic is a complete lack of faith in your ability or the ability of anybody else to protect you or help you in what you are doing.

People panic in different ways. Just look at the members of your family. Have you someone who goes very quiet when faced with something daunting? Is there someone else who is emotional when they are stressed? Is there someone who bursts into tears, becomes angry, silly or over-anxious? Is there someone who slams doors, breaks toys or thumps another member of the family? Have you someone in your family who develops headaches or always feels sick?

It is all right for your children to see you panicking and working through it. Do you panic when:

- you lose your keys?
- you are stopped for speeding?
- your children refuse to do what you ask?
- guests are coming?
- you have to go to Parents' Night?
- your children have homework you can't do?
- you can't get your printer to work?
- your children are in trouble?
- your children have a test or an exam?

Do you panic because:

- you think you should?
- you've run out of time?
- you don't know what to do?
- you're lost?
- you failed last time?
- you feel friendless?
- you don't think you're up to the task?
- you think you will be blamed?

Children panic too. They can panic when:

- they break something
- they hear adults argue
- they feel threatened

- ◆ they think they have no friends
- ◆ they think they have got something wrong
- ◆ they think they have let you down
- ◆ there is a test or an exam
- ◆ they have lost something

Children panic because they:

- ◆ feel unsupported
- ◆ think they will get your sympathy
- ◆ think they will be in trouble
- ◆ don't know what to do
- ◆ don't understand what is going on
- ◆ can't explain
- ◆ think no one will understand
- ◆ think no one is interested

In this chapter you will learn how to help your children over-come panic. You will learn how to believe in yourself and your ability to use whatever is available to help your children achieve their goals. Sometimes you can draw on your own resources and sometimes you will need to look elsewhere. You will learn to remember times when you have been successful. You will stay calm and use your common sense to get as far as possible. When you learn how to overcome panic yourself, you will be able to help your children overcome panic themselves. They will feel calm, interested in setting goals, pleased with their achievements and confident that, with effort and thought, they will be able to do their best. They will feel calm, interested in why something went wrong and able to cope when life isn't perfect.

How panic can interfere with success

Panic can be harmful.

It can take over. Family life becomes miserable. The 'panicker' is living a nightmare.

PANIC CAN CAUSE FAILURE.

The work for the exam is not done as well as it could be, if at all.

PANIC CAN BE LIMITING.

Children avoid exams so their educational opportunities are limited. They feel their sense of worth is tied up with the exam and they can't bear feeling judged. If they feel they won't succeed they won't try.

PANIC CAN CREATE PROBLEMS.

Some children take quite extraordinary measures to avoid exams or tests because they can't bear the panic that they feel when the day they dread arrives.

PANIC CAN BE FASHIONABLE.

A friendship group can suddenly become a place where children are only welcome if they are panicking. Peer pressure may only last as long as children are with the peer group or it can take them over completely. If it takes them over completely it will lead to disappointing results.

PANIC CAN BE NEGATIVE.

Parents can be sucked into their children's panic and react in an immature way. Parents need to remember they are adult. It is not unusual to hear groups of parents talking excitedly together about how stressed they are over their children's exams. They try to outdo each other with their levels of stress.

PANIC CAN BE TURNED INTO SOMETHING POSITIVE.

Parents can work out a way of helping their children. Parents can recognise when they might need support themselves.

There are strategies parents and children can use that will mean that every testing situation can be met in a balanced way. Parents can teach their children to be at ease when they are being tested. Parents can learn to be at ease when their children are being tested. People who can remember how they were successful before will know how to be successful again.

Tried and tested – parent power prevents panic!

Children can use panic as a way of stopping or avoiding any pressure. The following parents found ways to help their children cope with panic. They showed love and care by helping their children find a new way of coping.

When Dawn panicked she became very clingy and would refuse to look at anybody except her mother. Her mum stopped being so protective and gently insisted that Dawn look at people who spoke to her.

When Michael panicked he would use baby talk and wouldn't join in at school. His dad decided to insist that Michael do what he was told at home.

When Rachel panicked she couldn't concentrate. Her mum began doing relaxation exercises with Rachel each night at bedtime.

When Elizabeth panicked she giggled. Elizabeth and her dad wrote a list of all the brave things she had done.

When Paul panicked he became withdrawn. His mum made a list of jobs he had to do before he could go out to play.

When Daniel panicked he started to be silly. When he was silly his parents spoke to him slowly and quietly.

When Joel panicked he was aggressive. His parents allowed him to join in at his own pace.

When David panicked he became depressed. His parents reassured him that they loved him.

When Sarah panicked she ate too much. Sarah and her mother agreed that she should eat half of whatever she took and no more for five minutes.

When Rani panicked he cried. Instead of worrying about his

crying his parents looked at what he had to do and guided him as he did it.

It can take several attempts before children let go of old habits but it can be done. Parents can do it most effectively.

The A–Z of overcoming panic

ATTENTION

When people are panicking their attention is not focused. Their minds are full of many things. You can help someone who is panicking by suggesting one thing they can do and complete. When children have been crying because they are upset and overwrought, suggest that they go and wash their face. This gives them something to do that is helpful and also possible. If your children are panicking on the day of an exam, suggest you check together that they have all the equipment they need. Learning how to pay attention to one thing at a time is important for overcoming panic in exams and tests.

BREATHING

A powerful technique for dealing with panic is proper breathing. Teach your children how to notice the air as they take it in through their nose and as they release it through their mouth. If we teach children to control their breathing so that they are taking in enough oxygen to help their brains function efficiently, they will think more clearly and overcome panic.

CONSCIOUSNESS

Teach your children to be aware of changes. Change is part of life. You get more out of life if you are conscious of change. If you are conscious of change you can decide what to do about it. Play a game where you change one thing in the room and your children have to work out what is different. Give everyone a chance to make a change. Your children will become more conscious of the world around them and less threatened by change.

Decision-making

When people panic they stop making any decisions or they make so many decisions that it is impossible to follow them through. Teach your children how to make decisions sensibly and you will teach them how to take charge of their lives. Children who haven't been taught how to make decisions become very passive or impulsive. Take as many opportunities as possible to involve your children directly in decisions. Make sure you limit the range of possibilities to something that is safe and sensible for the age of your child.

Experience

Experience helps you learn how to deal with panic. The more decisions you make, the more experience you have of the consequences of any of your decisions. Experience tells you that your decisions are not always right. Sometimes your decisions will sort out the whole problem and sometimes they won't. Sometimes your decisions will create an entirely different problem. You don't always have to be right. Experience teaches you that some decisions you thought weren't going to be any good actually turn out surprisingly well.

Explain

Children need practice in explaining. Children will improve if they are given help. If your children are trying to explain something to you, give them questions that will help them get the whole story out. Give them a chance, when they have worked out the whole explanation, to tell it to you or to someone else. If children are to succeed in exams and tests they need to understand explanations and give their own explanations. They need to work out what they are being asked to do.

Figuring out

Teach your children to figure things out. You will be teaching them how to use what they know and find out what they don't know. When people figure things out, they let go of all the things they have been doing and clear a space in their mind to work with the new information. Panic comes about because we try to put new information into a mind that is already full. When we can't handle the information overload, we think we can't handle the problem. Teach your children how to figure things out. If you are having a picnic, let your children figure out what needs to be taken. When making a cake they can figure out how to decorate it. When wrapping a present they could figure out how it can be done.

Guessing

When people guess which lottery numbers will win them millions they are guessing in the dark. The rewards may be great but may also be nothing. In most cases in life we can make guesses which are based on things we know even if we can't remember them properly. As soon as we make a guess like this, there is a chance that we can find the answer. When helping your children with homework or revision, encourage them to have a guess if they don't know. When you hear their guesses you know where you need to start to help them. Children who can guess in exams and tests, when they are not certain, have a crucial strategy for success. Children need to learn that, although it is reasonable to guess wildly sometimes, in exams and tests a thoughtful guess is likely to be better.

Honesty

Panic often comes from pretence. If children learn that honesty is the best policy they will stop panicking. If they know that everyone makes mistakes, leaves things out and forgets something important, they will be calm when it happens to them. They will feel confident that the problem can be sorted out. Every so often make sure members of the family tell each other something that went wrong rather than pretending that they never make a mistake.

IDEALS

Ideals are a strong motivator. People with ideals may be panicked on the way to fulfilling them but they probably won't abandon them. They know panic is temporary. They will look for ways of making sure the ideal happens. When they panic they will deal with the panic, let it go and replan. Ideals can take years to become real. When you have an ideal you learn to recognise and appreciate whatever is happening. Idealists recognise that a measured rate of progress will eventually lead to success.

IDEAS ARE NOT THE SAME AS IDEALS

Damien's idea of a man was that he should own a car, have his own flat, wear designer clothes and have a job that paid him a lot of money. Damien was immature. As a teenager he thought manhood would be the solution to his problems. Damien took on no responsibilities in his teens. He thought all the things that mattered could be bought. He had no idea that if he wanted a job he would have to have some skills to sell. He just thought, 'Men are paid; when I am a man I will be paid. If I am not paid as a man I will not work.' Damien did not understand how to build towards an ideal of manhood. He expected things to be easy and instant and they weren't.

William had a difficult time as a teenager, but he had an ideal. His ideal was to be successful as an adult. He went to night school. He took on low-paid work where he could get experience and he gradually built up his credentials. He had no ideas about what he should have as a man but many ideas about what he could do. He was prepared to measure his progress in small changes. He was aware that changes in him would lead to maturity. He

didn't expect things to be easy and he didn't give up if
there was a setback.

JIGSAWS

Teaching children how to do jigsaws means you are teaching them:

- how to cope with sorting things out
- how to classify when they select the edge pieces and the corners and leave the rest for later
- to observe detail so they can find pieces that match
- a system for building up something large from lots of little bits
- to pause, reflect and think
- how to motivate themselves by being pleased as they make progress as well as with the finished jigsaw

KNOWLEDGE

Teach your children the importance of knowledge. Help them become aware of how you have acquired knowledge. It is liberating for people to know that everyone has to learn. When your children are learning something they will remember that learning takes time, even for people who seem to know so much. Children need to realise how they have changed as a result of knowledge. Then they will be motivated to learn more. It is important to share with your children recollections of what you and they have learnt today, this week, this year. Knowledge is power and effort is the fuel that generates the power of knowledge.

LETTING GO

Panic happens when we hold on to ideas whether they work or not. We leave no room for awareness. We are closed off. We hold on desperately to what we believe, even if it makes us unhappy. Our idea might be that we are always right or we are always wrong. If we learn how to let go of ideas we have a chance to see what is really happening. When we see what is really happening we can see how we can choose to do something that will stop the panic.

MEMORY

Teach your children to use their memory and you will give them great riches. Memory is the key to overcoming panic. Every child needs to know that their memory matters. Some children as old as eight don't know where they live, what their telephone number is or the date of their birthday. They don't have a learning difficulty but they do find learning difficult because they don't know that memory matters. Facts about yourself committed to memory are like hooks that can hold more facts. In modern society many children do not need to use their memory to survive. Someone else feeds them, reminds them to wash, packs their bag, takes them wherever they need to go and brings them back. When they do find themselves in a situation where they are expected to know what to do, because they have done it before, they panic or look blank. They should have committed some details to memory so they could use them again. How can children like this have self-esteem? They have been denied the knowledge and the skills that allow them to fend for themselves. Children have self-esteem when they know they can cope with those things that are expected from a citizen of their age and ability. They can't have self-esteem if they don't believe in themselves. They can't believe in themselves if they can't do those things they should be able to do alone.

NATURAL

Some people think panic is natural. Some people think panic is immature. Some people think there is an alternative to panic. The people who think panic is natural don't realise that panic is understandable but unhelpful. It is a stage that interrupts clear thinking. The people who think panic is immature may never have experienced a situation that they felt they couldn't handle. People who think there is an alternative to panic know that whatever is happening they can remember to separate themselves from it. They know that whatever is happening will pass and they will probably learn something positive from the situation. How you react to a difficult situation depends on your perception, knowledge and experience. Few people are mature in every situation. Panic can arise whenever we have expectations of ourselves that we cannot achieve. It isn't natural to have unrealistic expectations. We all have them and are gripped by them and advertisers play on them but they are not natural. We can choose to get the skills that will mean we are free of them. The most important skill is relaxation.

OBSERVATION

Teach your children how to observe what is really happening at any moment and you will teach them to overcome panic. Some children who feel they have no friends are so panicked by their dread of loneliness that they actually reject children who are trying to make friends with them. They are so overwhelmed by the belief that no one likes them that they look inwards to the memory of past rejection rather than outwards at the friendliness that is being shown. They miss the chance to change the situation where they feel rejected.

In exams children who panic can fail to read the question properly or answer the question that has been asked. They are so convinced that they already know what to expect that they don't pick up the information that is on the paper to help. Sometimes that information will tell them what to do and other times the information might act as a trigger for their memory. Encourage your children to tell you what they can see, when you are in the car, doing homework, having a picnic or waiting for an appointment. Gradually they will improve their ability to see what is around them or in front of them.

Preparation

Positive preparation prevents panic. Panic can happen because we are not prepared. We think we need something else. We need to learn to step back, look at the situation and think about what needs to happen next. Children need to recognise what needs doing. They need to decide the order for action and then work through it. They need to know that at any point their plans might have to be changed. People who learn how to plan positively will make the best of whatever events are happening in their lives. Make sure your children pack their own school bags, swimming bags, etc. – an exercise in preparation.

Questioning

You can help your children succeed in exams and tests if you teach them to use questions well. Questions give them the chance to show what they know and find out what they don't know. Children who use questions well develop the ability to reflect on what is being said in lessons and will think when they ask a question. They will question themselves as they are working, checking, exploring and developing their work. Children who can respond to questions in class can increase the amount of learning all children in the class get.

Some children are frightened of answering questions or asking them. Others think if they ask a question or answer one they will lose their status. Other children do not realise how much interest, knowledge, humour and excitement can be unlocked by entering into learning based on questioning.

Relaxation

Real relaxation while working is the key to success in exams and tests. The secret of real relaxation is mentally to take yourself out of the situation that you are involved in. You will create a space and clear your mind before you start the next activity. All your attention can then go towards what needs to happen next. You will feel refreshed and you will have lots of energy.

One person's relaxation can create another person's panic. Seeing your children relax in front of the TV set when they should be doing their revision can create panic for you. Time is running out, not enough has been done and there are no signs that revision is on the agenda. It could be your children are avoiding what needs to be done by 'vegging out'. They will assure you that this is an important activity that will help them to work. You feel they haven't got time to relax like that. They need to be getting on with their study. Sort out your own panic before you attempt to sort out the situation. Then you will see clearly how to help your children get back to their work.

Strategies

Effective strategies mean that you can make the most of any opportunities in your life. Tests and exams are opportunities and if you teach your children strategies for dealing with them, any panic they feel will be temporary. Adults know the importance of strategies to cope with unexpected developments. One of the simplest strategies is what to do if the family group gets split up while shopping. Your strategy might be to meet at the car, meet at the front door of the store or go to the information desk. The more strategies your children have developed to cope in different situations, the less need they will have to panic. Strategies need to be updated. Sixteen-year-olds could need new strategies to those that worked when they were nine.

Thinking

Panic means thoughts that are out of control. Thinking means putting in some structure, rearranging ideas and using all your senses. Thinking is about remembering things that might be helpful and working out what to do next.

Unravelling

Panic can happen when you feel as though everything is un-ravelling around you. You don't feel there is anything that can stop the whole thing from becoming, at best a mess, and at worst chaos. Many situations unravel every day. But mostly we know how to sort out the problem. You cook some potatoes and they boil dry. A child faced with this situation might panic and cry or panic and throw the pan away. An adult might want to cry and throw the pan away but instead rescues unspoilt potatoes and sorts out the saucepan.

Help your children cope when something begins to unravel by teaching them that things can go wrong for everyone. Include them in helping to sort problems out. Building blocks and construction toys give children experience in making things in different ways and sorting out how to correct their model if it is not the way they want it. Children who think the questions in spelling or tables tests are going to come in a particular order can panic if the order is changed. Their belief that they know what to do starts to unravel. Encourage children to learn information so that they feel confident they can answer the questions in any order.

Vocabulary

The way people often help each other to cope with panic is through words. People use words to describe how they feel, what they need, where they have been and what they have seen. Teach your children how important words are. The more children realise how important words are, the more interested they will be in having new words to use. Playing Scrabble with a dictionary alongside to check for words is an ideal way to acquire new words.

Work

The more children can pace their work the less likely they are to panic. If your children make a timetable of what they are going to do they will realise how to fit the activities they have to do into the time available.

You

You will be able to overcome your panic and your child's panic if you decide panic is not productive.

Zany

If you can enjoy the unexpected, be delighted when you notice something amusing and expect to see humour in the world around you, your panic will be a thing of the past – probably.

CHAPTER 19

RESOLVING CONFLICT AND DEALING WITH CRITICISM

Resolving conflict

Family conflict can come from disagreements, disappointed expectations and disputes. Some of these conflicts will have an edge and anyone involved will feel bruised. Other conflicts will be over quickly and a compromise found. Occasionally conflict will escalate to the point where there is family breakdown.

Up until the age of sixteen conflict with children comes from:

- their desire or determination to do something that you don't want them to do
- their equally strong desire not to do something that you want them to do

Families need to learn how to deal with conflict. Conflict is part of life and people who cope with conflict successfully have considerable advantages over those who don't.

Handling conflict

Conflict can be handled positively in several ways.

Roger should have been studying for his end-of-year exams but his friends wanted him to go out car washing with them. Roger's parents wanted to be sure that he would do enough study. Roger gave them a plan of his studies and showed them how he would have time.

THE SITUATION IS SIDE-STEPPED IN ORDER TO MAKE PROGRESS

Joanne had a spelling test and could not remember any of the words no matter how much her mum tried to teach her. Joanne was getting distressed but her mum didn't want to give in. They did a relaxation exercise and afterwards Joanne's dad took over.

LET THE ISSUE GO TEMPORARILY

David had some difficult coursework. He struggled with it over the weekend and was making no headway. He was bad-tempered and picking fights with everybody. His dad suggested he leave it and the family went out for a walk. The next day David talked to his teacher and got help over his difficulty with the work.

Conflict is a part of growing up but many parents feel that in a perfect family, conflict shouldn't happen. They feel that if their children show any displeasure or discomfort then the situation needs to be sorted out, so that the displeasure or the discomfort is dispelled. The danger of parents always compromising is that they lose their role as parents.

Firm parenting

Children need firm parenting. Firm parenting means giving children limits and teaching them how to cope with the life that they are living. By giving your children clear direction you will help them achieve the best out of every situation they encounter.

If children aren't given clear direction they feel they can endlessly challenge and undermine situations they find themselves in. This can result in children being left out, held back, excluded, ignored or failing. Children who think they can push the boundaries all the time are exhausting. Children who haven't learnt limits can feel terribly upset when they are rejected. They think other people are unfair and don't understand that, unless they work out why they are being rejected, the problem will happen wherever they go. It is understandable that people want to reject children who have not learnt limits.

Parents who give clear limits give their children opportunities. Parents who don't give limits take opportunities away from their children.

Conflict over exams

Parents, whether they like it or not, are going to be parents of children who are to take exams or do tests.

Good results depend on many factors. When some children are supported they will do brilliantly. Other children can be given the same support but for some reason it just doesn't work.

At certain times, exams and tests can dominate family life. Conflict will arise unless families find a way to protect some time to relax.

Pressures of time

Growing up is a busy time. Children have to learn how to look after themselves. They have to learn how to make friends. They have to learn how to be safe and they have to go to school. Conflict with parents can come when parents see quite clearly that exams and tests are important but their children don't agree. Arguments can start about how much time should be spent studying and what should be stopped while revision is going on. The greatest conflict is when children won't study at all.

Students may not want to study because:

- they want to appear cool
- they don't know what they should be learning – they don't know how to sort it out and no one has told them
- they won't let the teacher help them
- they are frightened of being picked on if they do well
- they don't know how to ask for help
- they don't know how to revise
- they have too many things to do
- they have decided that they mustn't be too clever
- they have panicked when they felt stressed and abandoned the work
- they think they have better things to do with their time
- they have modelled themselves on the wrong person

Plan for the long term

Getting your children to take exams seriously and understand their importance is not something that can be done overnight. It is not something that can happen in one discussion. You have to demonstrate the sort of commitment that has to be made. You can do this by helping with homework, helping with revision and arranging family activities so they don't interfere unduly with opportunities to study. In this way you will be providing the conditions which give your children every opportunity to achieve success. You will be organising your life to give them the chance to study. They can organise their lives to make use of that chance.

If you have tried to make space for study and your children are still not interested then you might have to be philosophical and mature. Keep a sense of balance. You might have to wait for your children to grow up or someone else to come into their lives who will show them that study is worthwhile. Keep your eyes open for other ways you may be able to support your children.

Take time to reflect if results are disappointing

When exam results come out children feel vulnerable, even if they have done well. Exam time is extremely emotional and flashpoints can occur without warning. There may have been no conflict before the exam but the results are disappointing. Tread carefully as you try to find out why there was a problem. When exam results are disappointing lots of parents worry that they should have done more to help their children. In fact students may not have done well because:

◆ they have missed so much while they were fooling around and they were too scared to admit it
◆ they have always got good marks for attainment but those good marks might have been for presentation
◆ they had thought they were the best so they hadn't bothered getting better
◆ they have irritated the teacher and missed out on the teaching that was available
◆ they are frightened of schoolwork when it gets difficult
◆ they have missed a building block in the subject that is essential for progress and no one has realised it
◆ they don't realise that, as they get older, answers take more thought and any assignment will take longer than it did in earlier years
◆ they have unrealistic expectations of how much work needs to be done
◆ they haven't been encouraged to attempt anything that is hard
◆ they haven't been taught how to cope with learning or doing something that is hard
◆ they are setting themselves unrealistic goals
◆ they have been accepted to do a subject when they haven't known the basics

Exam results can help your children organise their study so that it will be more effective next time. All is not lost. Don't get into an argument about missed opportunities or a poor result. There are many directions students can take to study successfully. As children get older they have more chances to study something in a way that interests them. Their motivation increases because they can see that their studies are leading directly towards a goal that they want to achieve.

Parents' Night and conflict

Parents' Nights are there to develop a partnership between home and school, but they can be very tricky. Parents might be anxious about how the school is dealing with their children. They might want to talk to the teachers about their concerns. The children's teachers might want to talk about the problems they are having with the children. This situation is ripe for conflict.

Conflict can be overcome if everyone is listening carefully, trying to understand each other's point of view and respecting each other's opinions. It is important for people to find ways of moving forward rather than defending a situation that should not continue. If teachers mention something about your children that they think is holding them back, ask how they think you could help at home. If you think there is a way the school could support what you are doing you could suggest it.

The secret of a successful Parents' Night is when the teachers and the parents can create a positive time to discuss children's education. Negative emotions have to be put aside.

Criticism and conflict

Parents are often good at seeing how to sort out the frustration between their children but not so good at sorting out the frustration between their children and themselves. Sometimes conflict arises because parents feel their children haven't tried their best.

Beware. Parents would be surprised how often children try to do their best but haven't really realised what they should be doing. Quite often the instructions children are given are not as clear as we might think. Children are expected to understand. If they make a mistake they are criticised for being lazy or naughty or not having listened. As a result children feel stupid or upset because they think they should have known what to do. Conflict starts. You feel frustrated. They feel let down.

Before you start to criticise their efforts, make sure your children knew what they should have been doing. If they have got something wrong, check what they thought they were doing at each step.

Frustration and conflict

Quite often we don't realise that we have not told our children what they need to do. We think they will have picked up the information. They don't respond in the way we want them to. We think that is deliberate. We think it is because they can't be bothered. They know it is because they can't. They get upset. You are so convinced they should know what to do that they believe you. They feel stupid and inadequate. Everyone feels frustrated.

Criticism and confidence

Being a parent can make you feel very vulnerable about whether you have the ability to help your children. You may feel worried and confused about what to do. You are not sure whether you should criticise your children. You know criticism can be constructive and you know it can be cruel. You have conflicting ideas about what to do to help. You would like to be your children's friend. You are worried that criticism might undermine the friendship.

Don't worry. Criticism can be constructive. Constructive criticism will give your children suggestions for how to have another go and the confidence to try.

When you are checking their work a pencil dot or question mark by an incorrect answer lets them know that they need to do a correction. A cross is meant to do the same thing but can feel crushing. Crushing criticism will leave your children feeling incompetent and unwilling to have another go. When a teacher said, 'What a shame, you haven't underlined your headings, which would have meant you got an A', she was being constructive. It was quite clear what needed to be done to improve the mark. If she had put a 'B' with the comment, 'Not good enough', the student could have felt crushed.

If you can compliment your children on what they have done they will feel encouraged to keep going. When your children are tidying their rooms it is a good idea to make a comment about how well the room is coming on. You could notice the books that have been picked up and make a comment about the improvements you can see. It is always better to acknowledge what has been done and avoid being angry because it isn't finished.

Criticism in a crisis

Criticism can be constructive if it builds confidence and destructive if it is unreasonable. Unreasonable criticism happens when parents feel emotional for whatever reason. When you are trying to help your children you are better to back off and say nothing if you are feeling overwrought and emotional. When you are emotional your judgement can be clouded. You can say things that, the minute you say them, you know would have been better left unsaid. If you catch yourself getting emotional then you are better to stop any further conversation until you feel calm.

Don't panic. Do not feel you have damaged your children if you have become emotional. We all forgive people we love when they are not perfect. Your children will forgive you in the same way as you would forgive them. Again and again.

Calming conflict

Children can get into conflict with one parent or one teacher. The situation can quickly get worse because neither child nor adult is given any help to sort out the conflict. In circumstances like this, other adults can be extremely helpful. They can suggest ways of breaking the deadlock. They can help both the adult and child find a way of resolving the situation together. Everyone needs advice sometimes to get some more ideas about how to cope with life more efficiently.

If you are a parent with the most responsibility or sole responsibility for your children, you are bound to want advice sometimes. Don't be embarrassed to use other adults who you feel could help. You could be an adult with lots of support at home but still want advice from outside.

Comparison and conflict

You learn a lot from watching other children. Most parents these days don't know lots of other children so whenever you get a chance to observe how children behave, you will get clues to the way your own children might develop.

Beware. If comparison isn't constructive and confidence building, try to avoid it. Conflict can come when parents watch other children and then compare them with their own children. Children can feel betrayed.

Don't panic. Most parents, at some point, will compare their children even though they know comparing one child against another can be very damaging. Most of us hear comparison as a judgement. We feel we are not as worthy as the person with whom we are being compared. You can make amends by finding a time to talk to your children about how well they are doing or how much they know, compared to an earlier time.

Parents' Night and comparison

Parents can feel concerned by the comparisons teachers make. As schools are required to teach children certain things at certain times, Parents' Nights are scheduled to pass information to parents about the progress of their children. The best information states clearly where children are against the average. Parents can feel hurt if their child is compared negatively to others in the class. Every parent wants to be sure that their children's education is being taken seriously and that the teacher cares about their children reaching their potential. Parents can cope with comparison providing there is going to be progression. Teachers should explain what steps are being taken in school to improve children's performance. This information is important for every parent.

Parents can feel devastated by the comparisons teachers make, particularly if the comparisons are negative. Teachers might describe your children as noisier, more talkative, less able to write ideas down, less able to get things right than other children in the class. If this happens to you, try to stay calm and seek clarity. Although being told information in this way can be devastating you can use it in a constructive way.

Comparison and clarity

Ask the teacher directly whether your children are the only ones presenting a problem or are other children causing difficulties or experiencing difficulties too. You need to find out whether:

◆ your children are different to everyone else in the class
◆ your children are the only ones that are different
◆ your children are part of a group that is different

You need to decide the following:

◆ is it *your* problem to sort out? Your child is tired on a Monday – get him to bed early on a Sunday. He is silly in the afternoon after he has had a blackcurrant drink with his lunch – pack water for him to drink. He is rude to the teachers – keep insisting that adults must be treated with respect
◆ is it the *teacher's* problem to sort out? He has poor concentration in class – find work he can manage. He can't see the board and so copies things down badly – move him to where he can see the board. He is not finding the History very interesting – get him to do some research and give a talk
◆ is it a problem you can sort out *together*? He doesn't get his work finished – keep him in at playtime. He doesn't get his work finished – send it home. He's disorganised – both of

you will work on it. At home he will clear the table. At school he will pack his own bag before he leaves the classroom

◆ is it a problem that is *beyond both of you?* Sometimes problems arise for children because of the way the school is organised. In the main you and your children's teacher can't change the organisation of the school but you can both help children cope so they succeed rather than sink

If the teacher tells you that other children are having the same difficulties as yours it will probably be because what is being taught is too difficult for that group of children. It could be that it is normal for children to find this particular piece of work difficult and they will get there in the end.

Comparison and commonsense

When you have collected the information you will be able to help your children because you will know the nature of the problem. Once you have got a complete picture you can decide what to do next. You might decide that the problems you're hearing about have more to do with the age of your child, the size of the class or the pressures on the teacher. You might decide to wait and just see how things develop. You might decide to try to solve the problem yourself. You might decide to get some advice from a book, a friend, a relative or an expert of some sort. Be careful whenever you talk to someone else about the situation. Keep weighing up what you know and what you need to know. Just keep using your commonsense.

Consult with care

Difficulties, tiredness and frustration are as much a part of parenting as pride, joy and a sense of a job well done. Parents are not irresponsible because their children have difficulties. Sometimes when you ask other parents whether their children are having difficulties like your children, they will make you feel embarrassed. They say their children aren't having any problems at all. You can feel a failure if other parents make you feel that you are the only person who has a problem with your children. Bear in mind you are only trying to help your children and you need information to do that. Even if you feel hurt by another parent's attitude you will know you have behaved responsibly. All children will meet difficulties at some point and most parents will meet a difficulty that they cannot manage to sort out alone.

Constructive comparison

THE BOY WHO LEARNT HOW TO GET MORE MARKS

John wrote a six-page essay for his English coursework. He got a poor mark. Peter wrote five pages and got a good mark. John thought he should have got more than Peter because his essay was longer. John's teacher helped him compare the two essays to see why Peter had got more marks. By comparing marks John learnt nothing but felt let down. By comparing the essays John could learn how to write a better essay and get a better mark.

If your children can learn how to see the benefit of comparison they will be able to work on improving their own performance. They will notice what qualities make their work different. They can begin to make changes for themselves. They will compare naturally and without feeling inadequate. They will be able to accept that people are different and not feel frightened of the differences.

Conflict and appearance

Conflict can be comical – especially if you're not involved. Many parents, without realising, want their children to be a carbon copy of themselves. They want their children to conform to their idea of what makes a good child. Some children expect their parents to conform to their picture of what a good parent is.

Where did you get that hat?

Kelly couldn't bear it when her mother came to collect her from school wearing a hat. She pleaded with her not to wear this hat in public, particularly in a public place if they were together. She was embarrassed by her mum's style.

You can't wear that!

When Luke took to wearing a grubby looking t-shirt with a screaming and bloody skull on the front his parents pleaded with him not to wear it on visits to his grandparents. Every Sunday there would be a battle of wills. Luke enjoyed his own style and couldn't see that it was of any interest to anyone else.

Conflict over style has probably gone on since clothing was invented. Don't despair and remember that some of the greatest fashion designers started out when they decided they wanted to be different.

Conflict and rebellion

Children rebel because it is a part of growing up. Some children seem to have a compulsion to establish their own identity. They may rebel only at school or just at home or everywhere. It is often difficult to discuss with them why what they are doing might be limiting their chances. They need to know they can be as big a rebel as they like providing they realise the consequences. If their rebellion interferes with their education then they can't expect to get the same results as people who have decided to conform.

People who rebel tend to think that:

- they should always speak their mind
- no one else should tell them what to do
- the course is no good
- everyone else is boring
- no one is noticing what exciting individuals they are

- they have missed so much they don't want to feel that they are not as good as others
- they don't know the benefits of going with the flow
- they don't know how to conform
- they should follow their heroes
- they don't want to be stereotyped
- it is right to be angry

When you are being a rebel you have tunnel vision. You think that anyone else who can't see your point of view is wrong. You can lose your sense of humour. Everything is deadly serious. You may, as part of your rebellion, actually conform to some set of ideals, dress or way of life you have seen somewhere else. You often only notice the negative ways of making a stand or getting a point across.

Rebel with reason

The most important thing you can teach your children about getting their point across is the importance of politeness. Although being rude might work in the playground or at home, in most places people listen if they feel the person talking to them is respecting them. People who are disrespectful run the risk of having their ideas and wishes disregarded.

Don't panic. Experience has shown that most people who rebel grow up to become functioning adults, particularly if their parents have been able to remain steady during the rebellious times.

CHAPTER 20

RELAXATION TECHNIQUES

Really relaxed and really successful

When people learn to relax, their lives change. If you learn to relax and you help your children learn to relax, they will have the key to fulfilling their potential. Relaxation is the key to clear thinking, efficient use of energy and self-belief.

Children who learn how to relax learn how to concentrate and how to focus. They learn when to be involved and when to walk away. Parents who learn how to relax know how to keep calm so they can help their children. They will avoid being sucked into their children's panic. They will remember they can help their children to become independent. Parents who stay calm will sense the best moment to offer help.

Becoming calm – useful in exams and tests

The simplest way to relax is to use your senses. You can do this sitting down, standing up or when you are in bed.

- With your eyes open or shut feel the weight of your body pressing down on the chair or the floor or the bed.
- Notice what you can hear.
- Notice what you can smell.
- Although you are aware of everything, let nothing disturb you.
- Be still.

- Notice your breathing and draw in fresh air to give your system more oxygen.
- As you deepen your breathing you will become calm.

Focusing – essential in exams and tests

Whatever you are doing you will do it most effectively if you are paying attention. The point where you pay attention is the point where you need to be working. If you are writing your name you are paying attention to the pen on the page. Look at where your pen touches the paper. Watch the letters as they appear. Even though your fingers are very close to your pen, keep watching what is happening on the paper. Children who learn to focus where their attention is needed learn how to block distractions. They are open to remembering what they know. In exams and tests, children who can focus have a powerful tool for giving their best.

Relaxation to bring success

When children learn to relax they overcome the effects of:

- trauma in its many forms
- self-doubt
- poor concentration

People who gradually overcome experiences that mean they under-achieve will do better in exams and tests.

In the following relaxation exercises the listeners are asked to picture things in their mind's eye. For some children this is very difficult to do and they may worry that while you are speaking they cannot see anything. Tell them not to worry. Tell them that simply listening to the relaxation and letting their mind hear the words, while they breathe deeply, will be very helpful.

Suggestions you can make to someone who is practising relaxation

CLEARING THE MIND

When you want to become very calm, picture a candle. The candle is lit and you can see the flame. As you look at the flame you see the gentle movement. Just let your mind rest on that picture.

When you want to help your children to relax, find a time and a place for you both. Relaxation exercises are very effective at any time. Whenever they are used they restore calm. A space is cleared in the mind. People of whatever age are able to cope with their life with greater ease.

Relaxation exercises can be done anywhere. If you can, choose a place that is comfortable where you will not be interrupted.

Your children can lie down while you read to them. Your first instructions to them will help them to release tension from their body.

Before every relaxation exercise

Begin by asking your children to take a few deep breaths. They may make a noise when they breathe in, so gently explain that the deep breaths they need to take can be taken quietly.

Count to ten while they lie still. Count steadily and slowly and they will breathe in and out steadily and slowly, picking up your rhythm.

To release tension, ask your children to tighten their feet and then let them relax. Then tighten their legs and let them go. Continue asking them to tighten and relax their stomach, their chest, their shoulders and their back. Ask them to squeeze their hands into two tight fists and then to let their fingers relax. Ask them to tighten the muscles in their face and then let them go. Ask them to lift their eyebrows up towards their hair and then to relax.

Read the relaxation exercise you have chosen in a gentle but audible voice. As your children are breathing deeply make sure you are also breathing deeply so you will be relaxed as you read.

When you have finished reading the relaxation exercise count back slowly from five, like this. Tell them that you are going to count back from five. ' Five . . . . Four . . . . . . Three – wiggle your fingers, Two . . . wriggle your toes and One . . . when you are ready, you can slowly open your eyes and sit up.'

A relaxation exercise for keeping on going

Imagine that you are sitting in a park. It is a lovely day and the sun is warming your back. There are other people in the park and you are watching them. A little girl is practising skipping up and down on the grass. She is not using a rope, she is just trying to get her feet to move in the right rhythm. You watch as she concentrates hard and manages to get a little bit better each time. Suddenly she stops and calls out to her mum to watch while she skips and hops back. You smile, her mum smiles and the little girl is delighted. You are reminded that there must have been a time when you couldn't skip and watching the little girl reminds you that all the things you can do now you had to learn once.

You watch a couple of skateboarders weaving their way through obstacles and sometimes trying to jump over them. Every so often they get a good run and sometimes they crash, but they never give up. They are serious and they are determined. They obviously believe it is worth putting a lot of effort into mastering this difficult skill.

Think of some other things that you can do that you must have learnt. It might be riding a bike, it might be swimming, it might be catching a ball, writing your name or doing sums. Remember how slow it was to learn how to keep your balance on your bike and how to stay up when you were swimming. Remember how often you dropped the ball before you learnt that you had to keep watching it. Can you remember the excitement you felt when you realised you could remember all the letters and get them in the right order for your name? Remember the last time you learnt something new in maths and realised you could get it right.

Take one last look at the people in the park. There is the little girl learning how to skip and there are the skateboarders practising. As you look at the people in the park, think about something that you are learning to do. You get up to leave the park. As you go, enjoy thinking of things you have learnt and things you can do.

Count back slowly from five while you take some deep breaths.

A relaxation exercise for getting on with it

Imagine something that you are supposed to do that you don't like doing. It could be tidying your room, clearing the table, taking the rubbish out, doing your homework, practising the piano or being nice to your brother or sister. Think about how tired and cross you feel when you are asked to do something you don't want to do. See yourself wandering around and wasting time, doing anything other than getting on with this thing you don't like doing.

Imagine that you are someone who hates taking plates from the table to the kitchen. Think about why you hate taking the plates away. Perhaps it is because the plates are too heavy for you to carry. Perhaps the table is too high for you to reach the plates. Perhaps you know there is nowhere to put them when you get into the kitchen. Perhaps it is just too hard and you can't work out how to do it. Perhaps you just don't think it is fair.

Imagine that you are a sensible person. You know jobs need doing and you are good at doing them. You know that if you collect plates of the same size together you can carry two out at the same time quite safely. Because you are a sensible person you know that if you concentrate on clearing the table you will do it fast. You know that if you help, everyone feels happy, and when you help other people they want to help you. Think about how nice it is as you move the things from the table quickly and efficiently. People are happy around you as they get on with their jobs and you feel grown up because people can trust you to do your bit. Think how you feel when you look at the table and know it is cleared because of your effort.

Hold on to the feeling that you are a capable person who can be trusted to see a job through.

Count back slowly from five . . .

A relaxation exercise for knowing you are not alone

Imagine that it is the weekend and it is a particularly special weekend because you are going away, overnight, with your best friend, for the first time. You and your friend have been planning it for ages. You are going with your friend's family to stay with their grandparents who live near the sea. Your bag is packed. You have pocket money and books to read and you can't wait. You have a new notebook and pen in your pocket, given to you by someone who loves you.

When you are picked up you give the people in your family a hug and jump into the car to set off on your adventure. At first you really enjoy the journey. You chat to your friend. People crack jokes and share sweets. But the journey goes on for a long time. You want to ask how much longer it is going to be but you think your friend's parents might think that is bad manners. You begin to feel a bit lonely. You put your hand in your pocket. You feel the notebook and pencil that you were given and the loneliness disappears.

Soon you arrive at the house by the sea. There are lots of new things to discover. You enjoy exploring the new place and meeting the new people. Whenever you feel lonely or uncertain, you can remember you have people who care about you. Whenever you are unsure, you can remember those people. You can remember the smile they give you when you are having fun together or when they see you after you have been away. You can remember the little things they do for you that they know will make you happy because they know you so well.

Let those warm and familiar memories fill your heart and

your mind and flow through your body. You will feel loved and confident enough to cope with any situation.

Count back from five, slowly . . . ..

A relaxation exercise to feel capable

Imagine you are ten years old. For you, being ten might be something that has already happened, or you might not be ten yet. You are at the park with your friend. You are having a great game. You are enjoying the space and other people in the park are feeding the ducks, playing on the swings or sitting down having picnics.

Suddenly you notice two children who are crying and seem to be looking for something. You and your friend go over to ask them what is wrong. They tell you that their puppy has run away and they have come to see if it is in the park. You offer to help them look and ask them what their puppy looks like and what it is called. They show you a photograph of their puppy.

In the distance you can see a family having a picnic. You can see that some of the children from the family are calling to a puppy. You go and investigate and sure enough it is the missing puppy. Everyone is so excited that the puppy has been found.

You go back with your new friends and the puppy to their house. Their mum is delighted that you helped them. You are pleased that there is a happy ending and that you were a part of it.

A relaxation exercise for forgiving yourself

This next relaxation exercise is one that will help you to cope whenever you are feeling stupid. Everyone feels stupid some-times and when you feel stupid you feel really dreadful. You might feel dreadful when you don't get such good marks as other people. You might feel hurt because someone else has said you are stupid. You might feel awful when you do some-thing silly. Just remember you are not stupid. No one is stupid. We sometimes make mistakes and we wish we hadn't. But mostly we do clever things. We think, we notice things, we are helpful to other people and we learn. Even if we don't get good marks in tests, we are learning all the time. We learn from our mistakes. Making a mistake doesn't mean that you are stupid.

Keep your eyes closed and think of a time when you made a mistake when you were trying hard to help. You might have dropped something. You might have spilt something. You might have broken something. Did someone help you sort the problem out and show you how to do it differently next time? If they did you were lucky. If they didn't, that is a shame. Everyone needs help sometimes. You are not stupid because you don't know. You are not stupid if you make a mistake. You are clever. Clever people use their mistakes to find out how to do things better next time.

Count back from five . . . ..

A relaxation exercise for finding something positive in a change

Imagine that you are sitting by the side of a pond. The water is still and it is a lovely day. As you watch the water a fountain begins to bubble up from the pond. The jet of water grows and grows until the fountain is quite high. Then you notice that each drop of water that falls from the fountain back into the pond is coloured. Instead of clear drops there are blue drops and red drops. There are green drops and yellow drops. There are orange drops and purple drops. And when the drops are back in the pond, instead of mixing together, each drop keeps its own colour. The pond becomes like a kaleidoscope of different-coloured drops of water.

Then, just as the fountain grew, it begins to disappear. It becomes smaller and smaller until it has gone altogether and the pond is still once again. Gradually the colours disappear too, but something else starts to happen. In the centre of the pond a lily flower begins to poke up through the water. Once it has broken the surface of the pond the flower slowly opens. The petals bend back until they are resting on the water. In the middle of this beautiful flower you can see the tiniest bird you have ever seen. As you watch the bird appears to grow a little bigger and a little stronger. You can see that the bird has feathers of all different colours. Some of the feathers are red and some of them are green. Some of the feathers are orange and some are yellow.

Suddenly the bird flies up from the lily and away from the pond. You watch the bird soaring across the sky. You see that where the bird flew there is now a perfect rainbow. A wonderful arc of red, orange, yellow, green, blue, indigo and violet. The bird has left behind the most beautiful rainbow for you to marvel at.

A relaxation exercise for starting afresh

Picture yourself walking up some wide stone steps that lead up to a big wooden door. You go through the door and find yourself in a large hall. There is no furniture in this hall and there are no other people. You are the only person there. You notice that all around the room on each wall are paintings, some large and some small.

You walk around and have a look at some of the paintings. The hall must be a gallery and the paintings have been put here for people to enjoy. As you look at the first painting you are surprised to find that it is actually a painting of you. There you are wearing some of your favourite clothes and looking very happy. You move on to the next painting to see what that is of and once again find yourself in the picture. This time there are other people in the picture as well, some at the front and some at the back. The whole scene is one of light and colour. The clothes people are wearing are bright and colourful. The sky in the painting is a wonderful shade of blue and the faces of all the people in the painting are happy. Just looking at the picture makes you feel good.

You move on past the next few paintings looking for yourself in each one. And there you are in each painting. Sometimes you are in the foreground and sometimes you are at the back of a group. Sometimes there is a picture of you on your own but mostly the pictures are of you with other people. Each picture is bright and cheerful and you feel delighted as you look at them.

But then you come to some different pictures. You can still see yourself in each painting but the colours are very drab and dreary. Where people before were wearing bright and cheerful colours they are now wearing dull greys and browns. Where people before looked happy and as if they were enjoying themselves they now look miserable, unhappy and uncomfortable. Instead of feeling pleased when you look at these paintings you feel very sad that someone has painted you and the people you are with in such a miserable way.

Then you spot, in the corner of the room, one of those artist's palettes with blobs of different-coloured paint around the edge. Next to the palette is a jar of paintbrushes. You have an idea. You take the brushes and the palette and you go to the dull and drab paintings. You paint out all the grey and black clothes. You replace them with clothes that are bright and cheerful. Where people have long, sad faces you change them so their faces are happy and pleased. You work on each miserable picture transforming it into a painting of bright colours, energy and happiness. Where skies in the painting are grey and overcast you make them blue and sunny. Where buildings look dilapidated you smarten them up with fresh, clean paint. When you have finished every unhappy picture you put the palette and the brushes back in the corner. You leave the gallery but as you go some other people are coming in. You stay near the door to see what will happen when they look at the paintings you have changed. As they go around looking at the work on the walls it is as if they are becoming happier and happier. They are laughing and talking in cheery voices. Their faces look pleased. You can tell they are delighted with everything they see. You go down the stone steps and you can still hear the happy voices of the people inside, enjoying every single colourful painting, and you feel pleased inside.

Count back slowly from five while you take some deep breaths . . . ..

A relaxation exercise for delighting in difference

Imagine you are standing outside some huge wooden doors. From the other side of the doors you can hear the sound of voices. Under the door you can see light. You turn the handles on the doors, push the doors open and look into the room. At first all you can see is the light. Hanging from the ceiling is a large chandelier covered in lots of little lights. The light from the chandelier is so bright that it takes your eyes a while to get used to it. Under the chandelier there is a huge round table. The table is covered with dishes and plates of food. When you look around the room there are groups of people sitting round small tables. They are chatting and eating and obviously enjoying the food and the company. Someone gives you a plate and tells you that you can take anything you want from the table. You turn to look at the table and realise there is so much food that even if you took the tiniest bit of everything that would be too much for you to manage. There is hot food and cold food. There is savoury food and sweet food. There are plates of meat and dishes of vegetables and bowls of fruit. There is party food like crisps and jellies.

You realise you will have to choose what you are going to have. To start with you walk around the table a couple of times looking at all the food and deciding what you might have. You take your time choosing what you want and when you have made your mind up you fill your plate. Then you turn to find where your friends are. They are waving to you and showing you the seat they have saved. When you get over to the table you notice the plates that other people have chosen. Their plates look quite different from yours. It is interesting to see what other people have picked. You start to eat and find the food really tasty and enjoyable. You are so pleased with what you chose. The party is great fun and you have a lovely time. You will have so many memories of the food and your friends, how different you are and how you enjoy each other's company.

Count back from five while you take some deep breaths . . .

A relaxation exercise to help children be happy to show what they can do

Imagine that you are on a small rocky island in the middle of the sea. You see in the middle of the island that there is a lighthouse. It is tall and white with a room made from glass on the top. As the day draws to a close and the light leaves the sky you notice that the light on the lighthouse has not come on. This is terrible. You feel worried that boats will not know the island is there. They might think they are lost because the light from the lighthouse is not telling them where they are.

You decide to investigate to see what has happened. You climb up to the door of the lighthouse and push it. The door opens and you step into a small room. The room looks comfortable with chairs and a table. Spiralling up from the middle of the room is a staircase. You start up the staircase knowing that it leads to the room where the light is. As you go up and round you can see some light coming from the room. Finally you step out into the top room and see straight away what the problem is. The light is on, the room is bright but when you look at the windows you see that they are all covered by thick and heavy curtains. It is the curtains that are stopping the light from getting out through the windows and doing the job it is meant for. You quickly draw the curtains away from the windows. You work all round the room clearing the curtains away from each window as you go. As you pull back the curtains the light floods out across the island and out to sea. You know that ships will be able to see the light. You know that the lighthouse is doing what it does well, lighting up the island.

You go back down the stairs to the room at the bottom. As you leave the lighthouse you can see the light sweeping over the island and out to sea. You feel pleased with what you have done and happy to see the light.

Count back from five . . .

A relaxation exercise for feeling you have something to offer

Imagine that it is night-time and you are in bed. You are trying to sleep but you can't. You twist and turn. You cannot seem to find a comfortable position or let your mind prepare for sleep. You are worried because there are lots of things that you think you have not done too well. You think about the events of the day. There were lots of good things that happened – a good game, an interesting conversation and a friend who had been kind and thoughtful. You try to keep these in your mind.

Your curtains are open and you can see the stars. At first you see them but not really. It is as though your mind is really only thinking about things that have happened or things that might happen. As you keep looking out of the window the stars become clearer. It is as if you are seeing them for the first time. The stars are so distinct. Some seem so near. You know that most of them are very far away. As you look you realise just how enormous the world that you are part of is. You start to breathe deeply and your eyes seem to be able to see more clearly all the time. It is as if there have been curtains on your eyes but these have opened as well as the curtains in your room.

As you watch you feel part of the world that you share with the stars. You feel a tremendous sense of peace as you continue to notice these remarkable signals from the sky. Everyone can see the same stars. They are always there if we look. Sailors have used the stars to guide them. Homeless people have used them to give light when they have needed it. Explorers have used them to find their way. Artists have tried to put the wonder of the stars into poetry and paintings. Your mind seems to clear. You are so tiny compared to what you can see. You feel the wonder of the universe. You seem to be so aware of how you can see the world and be part of it. Your mind seems to have grown. You want to make your world and the world you share with others better. Your body feels light. Everything about you seems light and bright. You feel confident. You know that when you wake in the morning you will wake ready to see your world clearly. You will know what you need to do to make your world better. You feel certain you can do whatever is needed.

Count back from five. Each time you breathe, see if you can think of one thing you can do to improve your world, the world you live in, the world you share with others, the world you share with the stars. Five, four, three, two, one. When you are ready, wiggle your fingers and toes, open your eyes and have a good stretch.